Pub 11,16

JAPAN

Roy B. Teele, University of Texas, Austin

EDITOR

Masamune   Hakuchō

TWAS 533

Masamune Hakuchō

MASAMUNE HAKUCHŌ

By ROBERT ROLF

University of Florida

TWAYNE PUBLISHERS
A DIVISION OF G. K. HALL & CO., BOSTON

Published in 1979 by Twayne Publishers,
A Division of G. K. Hall & Co.
All Rights Reserved

Printed on permanent/durable acid-free paper and bound
in the United State of America

First Printing

Library of Congress Cataloging in Publication Data

Rolf, Robert.
Masamune Hakuchō.

(Twayne's world authors series ; TWAS 533 : Japan)
"Titles of Hakuchō's works cited": p. 156–57
Bibliography: p. 165–66
Includes index.
1. Masamune, Hakuchō, 1879–1962.
2. Authors, Japanese—20th century—Biography.
PL811.A8Z85   895.6'8'409   78-27532
ISBN 0-8057-6375-9

Contents

About the Author

Robert Rolf received a Bachelor of Arts degree in Japanese from Indiana University and Master of Arts and Doctor of Philosophy degrees in Japanese literature from the University of Hawaii. He is Assistant Professor of Japanese language and literature at the University of Florida; he was formerly Instructor of Japanese and Chinese at Duke University. He has written articles on several modern Japanese novelists, and has lived a total of five years in Japan.

Preface

In 1898 the nineteen-year-old university student Masamune Hakuchō (1879–1962) led an austere Christian life, rising early each morning for an hour of Bible reading. By 1910, however, the noted nihilistic novelist Hakuchō, in the vanguard of the Naturalist literary movement then at its height, held that belief was passé. In 1927 Hakuchō, one of Japan's leading literary critics, could state that he neither believed in the Christian God nor even liked its believers.

By the 1950s, however, disillusioned with literature and consumed with philosophical doubts, the respected septuagenarian essayist Hakuchō speculated whether he would call upon Christ when he died. At last, on his deathbed, the weak, tired old man Hakuchō joined in the prayers of the daughter of the man who had baptized him sixty-five years earlier, and died a Christian on October 28, 1962.

Hakuchō was a religious writer: a novelist, critic, playwright, and essayist who considered the question of doubt versus belief usually from the point of view of the skeptic. He was an influential literary figure during most of his life, although his works were seldom popular successes. Today, more than fifteen years after his death, there is considerable critical interest in him but he is not widely read.

That is regrettable, for his works treat timeless philosophical problems with intelligence and complexity. Although he is forever labelled (and at times thus dismissed) as a Naturalist, because of his close association with that late-Meiji literary movement, his works are surprisingly contemporary. He grapples with questions that, although perhaps ultimately of sphinxian unfathomability, will always occupy a central position in the serious literature of the world. Specifically, Hakuchō is concerned with the nature and meaning of human existence. Hakuchō seldom backs away from these fundamental philosophical issues. Whatever our opinion of his literary skills (and examination of such neglected areas as his plays reveals they are considerable), the earnestness and intelligence of his philosophical probing is never in doubt.

I first examined Hakuchō's works in writing a doctoral dissertation on Japanese Naturalism. I became intrigued by Hakuchō, the Christian turned atheist turned Christian again, a "realist" whose stories and plays are filled with apparitions, bewitchings, and surrealistic distortions of reality. I discovered (a bit too late for my dissertation) that Hakuchō, not Naturalism, should be my subject. Thus, other than Chapter 1 and much of Chapter 3, this study covers mostly different ground from my dissertation on Naturalism.

Hakuchō's career spanned more than six decades; he was extremely prolific. Rather than attempt the impossible task of mentioning every Hakuchō story, I will treat, in as much depth as space allows, a small number of works, about twenty-five stories and ten plays. These were chosen to facilitate discussion of Hakuchō's literary style and, above all, of the philosophical content of his writing. Undoubtedly some deserving works have been omitted, for which I must apologize. Also, inasmuch as this is a study of Hakuchō the author, my discussion of Hakuchō the critic is merely a brief introduction to that aspect of his career.

The opinions and accuracy of this study are entirely my own responsibility, but many people and institutions have been of valuable assistance. I would especially like to acknowledge the constant and immeasurable help of the Editor, Roy E. Teele. Also, Matsumura Hikojirō, a leading actor, and Noda Yūji, the director, of the Tokyo theatrical troupe *Kaze,* were of great help by providing valuable information, opinions, and encouragement in many conversations and letters.

Professor James T. Araki of the University of Hawaii read an earlier version of Chapter 5 and offered many useful suggestions; he was also an invaluable member of my doctoral dissertation committee. The chairman of that committee was Professor Valdo H. Viglielmo. I am extremely grateful to Professor Viglielmo not only for his expert guidance as dissertation committee chairman but also for first introducing me to Hakuchō's writing in 1969, while I was a student at Hawaii. I am also grateful to the other members of the committee: University of Hawaii Professors Hiroko Ikeda, Daniel Stempel, and Yukuo Uyehara. Professor Ikeda has also kindly sent materials relating to Hakuchō on various occasions, as has Thomas J. Cogan, doctoral candidate at Hawaii. Professor Kano Keiko of Chikushi Jogakuen Tanki Daigaku in Dazaifu has been of important last-minute help in looking at parts of several of my translated quotes. Oda Minoru, Professor of English literature and chairman

Preface

of the Department of Foreign Languages, Fukuoka University of Education, helped immensely by checking the accuracy of my translations in Chapters 5 and 6.

I am indebted to the cordiality and cooperation of the staffs of the libraries of Duke University and the University of Florida. My studies also benefited from a University of Florida Humanities Council Summer Research Grant in 1976. Lastly, I am exceedingly grateful to the faculty and staff of the Fukuoka University of Education for their inexhaustible hospitality and unflagging assistance.

ROBERT ROLF

Fukuoka

Chronology

1879   Masamune Tadao (pen name Hakuchō) born on March 3 in Honami village in Okayama Prefecture.

1879– Childhood in Honami; impressed by Buddhist tales told to
1893   him by his grandmother; exposed to Christian notions through American textbooks used in primary school; receives classical Chinese education for a year and a half.

1894   Visits Okayama City where he is influenced by American Protestant missionaries; increasing familiarity with Christianity.

1895   Considerable reading in Honami, especially of the works of Uchimura Kanzō.

1896   In Tokyo for several months, attends Uchimura's lectures on Carlyle, increases knowledge of Western literature; enters Tokyo Semmon Gakkō (later renamed Waseda University).

1897   Baptized by his pastor Uemura Masahisa.

1898– Living austere Christian life; increasingly under the influ-
1899   ence of Uchimura Kanzō.

1900   Begins to drift away from Uchimura and Christianity.

1901   Graduates from Waseda; abandons Christianity; under the tutelage of Shimamura Hōgetsu, he writes his first literary criticism.

1902– Translates English versions of Western literature, including
1903   the *Iliad* in 1903.

1904   Begins career as a drama critic having joined staff of *Yomiuri Shimbun* in 1903; first fiction, "Solitude," appears in November, 1904.

1905   Becoming inclined toward realistic fiction owing to the example of the *Doppo-shū* by Kunikida Doppo.

1906   Resumes writing fiction, including "Discord and Harmony," "The Second-story Window," and "Old Friend."

1907– Gains first critical recognition with Naturalistic story
1911   "Dust" (1907); one of leading participants in the Naturalist literary movement, writing "Whither?" (1908), "Hell"

(1909), "Wasted Effort" (1910), "Faint Light" (1910), and "Clay Doll" (1911); marries in 1911.

1912– Naturalism declines, writes first plays *White Wall* (1912) and
1916 *The Secret* (1914); often writes newspaper serials; stories include "By the Inlet" (1915) and "The Smell of the Cowshed" (1916).

1917– A period of psychological dissatisfaction and ennui; artistic
1920 impasse; attempts unsuccessfully to resettle in Honami (1919–1920), after six months returns to Kantō area.

1921 After moving many times finally settles in Oiso, begins copious reading and considerable literary activity; key short story "Illusion" (1922).

1924– In addition to fiction ("I Killed a Man, And Yet," 1925),
1927 very active as literary critic ("On Dante," 1927) and as playwright; plays include: *Shadows* (1924), *The Joys of Life* (1924), *Beyond the Clouds* (1925), *Spring at Azuchi* (1926), and *Mitsuhide and Jōha* (1926).

1928– Thirteen-month tour of Hawaii, America, and Europe.
1929

1930– During this period important mainly as literary critic; father
1936 dies (1934); play *Iwami Jūtarō* (1935); "thought and real life" debates with Kobayashi Hideo (1936); travels to Sakhalin, Korea, and China (1935) and Russia, Europe, and America (1936–7).

1937– War years: steady decline in literary output; mother dies
1945 (1942); story "Early Summer This Year" (1943); evacuee in Karuizawa (1944–1945); Tokyo home destroyed in air raid (1945).

1946– Very active: essays ("History of the Rise and Fall of Natu-
1952 ralist Literature," 1948; "Uchimura Kanzō," 1949), stories ("Escape from Japan," 1949–1950, 1953), and the play *Capture the Angel* (1947); awarded Japanese government's Cultural Medal (Bunka Kunshō) (1950).

1953– Increasing disillusionment with literature, continued reli-
1957 gious speculation; story "Nobunaga of Honnōji Temple" (1953); plays *Ejima Ikushima* (1953) and *A Death-like Peace* (1957); collection of essays *Doubt and Faith* (Kaigi to shinkō) appears (1957).

1958– Deaths of brothers Atsuo (1958) and Ritsushi (1961); stories
1961 "Autumn of This Year" (1959) and "Elder Brother Rii" (1961); preoccupation with prospect of own death; awarded

Yomiuri Prize for Literature (1960) for collection of stories *Autumn of This Year* (Kotoshi no aki) (1959).

1962　Delivers speech "Sixty Years of Literary Life"; asks Reverend Uemura Tamaki (Uemura Masahisa's daughter) to conduct his funeral; hospitalized with pancreatic cancer, comforted by Uemura's prayers; deathbed reconversion to Christianity; dies on October 28.

1963　Formation of theatrical troupe "*Kaze,*" which specializes in performing Hakuchō's plays.

1965–　Hakuchō's *Complete Works,* edited by Nakajima
1966　Kawatarō, published in thirteen volumes by Shinchōsha.

CHAPTER 1

Hakuchō's Life

I Childhood

MASAMUNE Hakuchō, whose original name was Tadao, was born in Honami in Okayama Prefecture on March 3, 1879. Honami is a small village on the Inland Sea of Japan. The Masamune family was an old one with a history of well over two hundred years, whose members had been engaged in the marine transport of lumber for five generations. Hakuchō's great-grandfather and great-great-uncle had been noted enthusiasts of *kyōka* (comic *waka*), haiku, *tanka,* painting, and calligraphy. For the following two generations, however, no male heirs were born. As a result, the Masamune family line was continued through two adopted sons until finally Hakuchō was born.

Being the long-awaited son, Hakuchō was pampered as a child. His grandfather, also without sons, had used his wife's barrenness as a pretext for keeping a mistress. As a result, Hakuchō's grandmother was all the more eager to pamper him. To complicate matters, soon after Hakuchō was born a son was born to his grandfather's mistress, too. Communication between the two houses ceased and Hakuchō lived in an atmosphere of embattled tension in the family house which looked out upon Honami Bay, the inlet that sometimes appears in Hakuchō's fiction.

As a baby Hakuchō sometimes fainted; as a child he was frail, irritable, and easily upset. He had a vivid imagination even as a child; he was often frightened in his sleep by dreams of monsters. Life with his bizarre, intense grandmother stimulated his imagination, too. When Hakuchō was about three, during the period of her greatest fears that her grandson would be poisoned by her husband and his mistress, Hakuchō's grandmother suddenly cut off her hair and began daily recitations of the Kannon Sutra before the family

15

Buddhist altar. She was often accompanied by her little grandson, who would try to mouth the words of the sutra, too.

At times Hakuchō would beg his grandmother to tell him stories, but he only remembered the frightening or macabre ones. One of Hakuchō's biographers, Ōiwa Kō, characterizes these stories as often containing "Buddhist superstition" (*bukkyōteki meishin*).[1] Another commentator, Yamamoto Kenkichi, sees the source of Hakuchō's attraction to the Bible to be his need to be freed by Christianity from the fear of Buddhist hell engendered in childhood.[2] As Hakuchō himself pointed out, his need for religion was linked with his fear of hell (and of death, too, perhaps) as seen in Dante's *Inferno* or his grandmother's Buddhist tales.

Finally, more sons were born to the Masamunes; there were nine other children, seven of whom survived childhood. The young Hakuchō was no longer the recipient of the exclusive attention of his parents and grandmother.

Hakuchō's first exposure to Christianity was in primary school, for the primary school texts were direct translations of American texts, which unwittingly introduced Christian notions. The Japanese government in its haste to introduce Western thought ordered books for use that not even Hakuchō's teachers fully understood. Students simply learned the alien material by rote in traditional fashion, although at the time Hakuchō began to wonder just what those books meant when they referred to such things as God (*kami-sama*) and the Lord of Heaven (*tenchi no shusai*).[3]

Hakuchō's father Uraji was the principal of an elementary school, the village head, and a moneylender. He was intelligent as well as practical, and noted for his skill in calligraphy. Uraji had been adopted into the Masamune family, but there were many businessmen and scholars in his own family. Hakuchō always felt his scholarly bent came from his father's side of the family.

Hakuchō's mother, Mine, was small, thin, tenacious, and proud of her samurai heritage. Her father had been a teacher of Chinese writing (*kambun*).

At fourteen, Hakuchō entered an old and venerable school, where for a year and a half he received a classical Chinese education. He left the school because he disapproved of the rough ways of the older students, although he was an affable boy in his teens.

II *Introduction to Christianity*

Hakuchō was first formally introduced to Christianity through the essays of Tokutomi Sohō and those appearing in the *Kokumin no Tomo* (The People's Companion) which he read when he was a student. His attraction to the Western faith was such that by the time he was sixteen he was attending sermons regularly although the church, to which he walked, was five miles away. He owned a Bible, which he read despite his inability to comprehend it fully.

An American Protestant missionary was gaining converts in Okayama City, and Hakuchō enrolled in his small mission school there. Although he had resisted the spell of the dynamic American when he first visited Honami to preach, Hakuchō soon came to feel that "the clear blue eyes of the American were eyes that saw Heaven."[4] In Okayama Hakuchō even found the missionary's "two blonde, blue-eyed daughters with their white skin to be visions of the Holy Mother."[5] From the beginning Hakuchō's interest in Christianity, although here obviously immature and sentimental, was bound up with his interest in the West.

Hakuchō was plagued by poor health at this time and this visit to Okayama in 1894 was originally undertaken in order to seek better medical attention. The trip provided him, however, with his first supervised Bible study and the beginnings of a closer association with the Christian religion. The school soon closed and Hakuchō went home to rest and regain his health.

Hakuchō spent most of the year 1895 at home reading. He read *Kokumin no Tomo,* the works of Uchimura Kanzō, and the literary periodical *Bungakkai* (Literary World), which attracted him to Western literature. He read a great deal of fiction, including such Edo writers as Bakin, Santō Kyōden, Shikitei Samba, Ryūtei Tanehiko, and Tamenaga Shunsui. He even read such Chinese classics as the *Shui Hu Chuan* (All Men Are Brothers) and the *San Kuo Chih* (The Romance of the Three Kingdoms).

Hakuchō was attracted more to the writings of the great Christian Uchimura Kanzō than to those of Tokutomi Sohō or any of the others he was reading. Hakuchō grew restless at home and longed to leave for a more stimulating environment. At first he considered going to Kyoto, but finally he decided that only modern Tokyo could provide him with the intellectual stimulation he craved. He felt Kyoto was too old a city.

Hakuchō left Honami for Tokyo in late February, 1896. In

Tokyo he learned for the first time of such giants of Western literature as Homer, Dante, Shakespeare, and Goethe. He was seized by
a strong desire to read as many of these Western classics as he
could. He began the preparatory course in English at the Tokyo
Semmon Gakkō (later to be renamed Waseda University). He next
found a church of his liking, attracted to it by the sermons of the
pastor, Uemura Masahisa.

He struggled with his poor health in the spring of 1896, but his
spirits revived when he took a summer course from Uchimura
Kanzō. Uchimura lectured on Thomas Carlyle that summer;
Hakuchō used the opportunity to get as close as he could to
Uchimura.

Soon after the satisfying experience of the summer course Hakuchō returned home to Honami where he suddenly fell ill. The country doctor who attended him was uncertain whether Hakuchō was
suffering from pneumonia or pleurisy. For several weeks Hakuchō
was near death and at this time he discovered that he could find
great consolation through prayer. Still weak, he returned to Tokyo
after over two months in bed. Full recovery took about half a year
from the fall of 1896 to spring, 1897. His illness had finally been
diagnosed as pulmonary tuberculosis; he moved to a temple to
recuperate.

Hakuchō studied the Bible while at the temple. When he had
regained his strength, he decided to be baptized. He hesitated and
deliberated before deciding to be baptized, for he did not want to
become a convert lightheartedly. He considered his baptism a
serious step.

In 1897 Hakuchō was baptized by Uemura Masahisa. He was
more under the spell of Uchimura than Uemura, however, whose
ideas failed to stimulate Hakuchō greatly, but Uemura then, as
always, provided a personal element to Hakuchō's relationship
with Christianity. Every Sunday he attended services at Uemura's
church, and he often visited Uemura's house, too, for private
instruction. For a couple of years after he was baptized Hakuchō
was a Sunday school teacher; he even considered becoming a
minister.

In 1897 Hakuchō was an insatiable reader of the writings and
translations of Uchimura, but his relationship with Uchimura was
of a different nature from his relationship with Uemura. As Ōiwa
Kō puts it, Uchimura moved Hakuchō toward the Christian faith in
the same way an actor might move his audience, but Hakuchō's

relationship with Uemura was of a different quality, being a special and intimate one between pastor and parishioner.[6]

With Uchimura there was only one-way communication, whereas with Uemura there was a reciprocal relationship, allowing Hakuchō to exchange information and opinions with his religious mentor.[7] Uemura was perhaps not as exciting an individual as Uchimura Kanzō, but he was a warm person who also possessed a keen understanding of literature.

Uchimura was losing the loyalty and support of some of his employees at his magazine, the *Tokyo Dokuritsu Zasshi* (Tokyo Independent Magazine), and this new attitude toward Uchimura, which was at least partially the result of his finanical problems, seems to have provided the occasion for Hakuchō to drift away from Uchimura, too. In the late 1890s, however, Hakuchō was still totally enamored of the thought, writings, and lecture style of Uchimura.

III *Literary Beginnings: Waseda*

From January, 1898, Hakuchō attended Uchimura's weekly lecture on such diverse topics as Carlyle, Dante, Goethe, American poetry, the Bible as literature, and Cervantes. Uchimura's lecturing style was low-key and undramatic, but sincere and effective. Uchimura opened Hakuchō's eyes to much of Western literature; in his diary there is soon mention of such writers as Dante, Milton, and Zola.

In 1898, Hakuchō got up early every morning and read the Bible from seven to eight, in addition to going to church services and prayer meetings. Living this austere life, he was only rarely able to see *kabuki,* one of the things that had brought him to Tokyo in the first place, for theater was considered sinful by most Japanese Christians of his day. He did go to *kabuki* performances occasionally, but the guilt he felt whenever he did made his visits infrequent.

At Waseda in 1899 Hakuchō's life (for the next two years) was little different from that of any other diligent student or zealous Christian. As time wore on, however, he began to undergo a profound change in his attitude toward life and religion. The first phase of this change seems to have been occasioned by a change in his opinion of Uchimura, whom he had hitherto regarded almost as the thirteenth apostle of Christ.

The beginning of this erosion of his admiration for Uchimura is usually cited as the cessation of publication of Uchimura's magazine in July, 1900. Uchimura had begun the magazine as a vehicle for his Christian thought in April, 1898. When the magazine failed, Hakuchō, who had read every issue, began to drift away from Uchimura, ceasing to read his works and to attend his lectures. After his graduation from Waseda in June, 1901, Hakuchō began to abandon religion.

Gotō Ryō discerns two definite reasons Hakuchō lost his religious faith. First, as Hakuchō himself later wrote, Christianity lost out to a youthful desire to follow his natural instincts and human nature. He came to feel that such worldly phenomena as the theater possessed greater reality than the Christian religion, which he came to regard as false. Also, as a young man in his twenties he could not adhere to the Christian prohibitions against *kabuki* and seeing prostitutes. He was at this time an avid reader of Chikamatsu Monzaemon's plays, and Gotō even feels that the love suicides of Chikamatsu may have fanned the flames of his interest in women.[8]

Secondly, Hakuchō stated late in his life that as a student he came to feel that Christianity was a severe religion, which held that since Christ carried a cross every believer had to carry one, too. He felt Christianity, despite the gentle tone of much of the Bible, was austere and expected one to ignore the beauties of nature, to be content with singing hymns in praise of the Lord.[9]

Hakuchō felt that the Christians of his day accepted an anachronistic religious philosophy, knew nothing of beauty, and made no effort to study the "new knowledge" (*shinchishiki*) or "serious subjects" (*gakumon*). Hakuchō was also incredulous at the Japanese Christian prohibition against drinking alcohol,[10] which is ironic in view of the fact that in later life he was to become a well-known teetotaler.

Hakuchō felt, in 1901, that he knew nothing of the world of industry and commerce or even of the geisha. He wanted to expand his horizons and to learn as much as he could of the "new knowledge." He found it regrettable that although he had been in Tokyo for five years, he knew well only the world of the student. He felt that contemporary novelists knew only a little of the world and that the poets viewed Japan as if "from the bottom of a well."[11]

The *Manchōhō* (Myriad Morning Report) newspaper was at that time encouraging works of fiction by young writers. Hakuchō submitted several stories, but with no success. When he compared his writings with those of his classmates, he found that his own were vastly inferior; he felt his style to be crude and his plots dull.

Hakuchō gave up as a writer and concluded he would have to be content with doing translation to earn a living. His classmates wrote under the direction of Tsubouchi Shōyō for their "circulating magazine" (*kairan zasshi*), but Hakuchō neither wrote for the magazine nor read it. He read Kōyō's works and Izumi Kyōka's "Yushima mōde" (A Visit to Yushima) (1899), and he concluded he could never write of geisha and the sensual life as they did and therefore could never hope to become a writer.

What launched Hakuchō's career as a writer, at least of criticism, was his inclusion while still a student at Waseda in Shimamura Hōgetsu's *"gappyō,"* or "critical symposia," in his weekly Yomiuri column *Getsuyō bungaku,* or "Monday Literature." Hakuchō participated in the *gappyō* from April to December, 1901. He was included primarily on the strength of his outstanding academic record at Waseda.

Hakuchō had become well known by 1901 for his considerable facility with English. Takayama Chogyū had enhanced Hakuchō's reputation by telling various members of the literary establishment how Hakuchō had at times pointed out Chogyū's mistranslations when Chogyū was lecturing at Waseda on English poetry. Hakuchō's ability to correct Chogyū's mistakes was probably a result of his familiarity with the Bible which facilitated his identification of the many biblical allusions found in English poetry.[12]

Hakuchō supported himself by translating from English in 1902. He translated from English versions of the *Iliad* and other classics, as well as from works by such writers as Honoré de Balzac. In 1903, Hakuchō secured a job as an "arts reporter" for the Yomiuri newspaper. The move began a new era for him, for he gained an opportunity to write, which would sharpen his narrative style.

IV *Literary Beginning*

In March, 1904, Hakuchō began drama criticism. In his knowledge of the technical aspects of the theater Hakuchō did not measure up to the established critics of his day. However, he did learn much from contact with such men.[13] As an outsider his criticism was generally impressionistic, but he was free to criticize where one more intimately bound up in the theatrical establishment might not dare to. His criticism often brought him abuse, but likewise it often brought him praise.

Hakuchō's career as a drama critic was to be brief but turbulent. In fact, he gave up drama criticism after about September, 1905, when he embarrassed himself in print by misinterpreting an innocent gift from an actor as an improper attempt to influence Hakuchō's opinion of an upcoming performance.[14]

Hakuchō's first short story, "Solitude," appeared in November, 1904. He took great pains in composing it and revised it many times, but it created no excitement whatsoever when it appeared. He was not satisfied with it either, although he could not identify the problem.

For the next several years Hakuchō's tastes drifted toward realistic fiction. The appearance of the *Doppo-shū* (A Doppo Anthology: a collection of stories by Kunikida Doppo) was one of the first of a train of events that led to the appearance of the *shizenshugi,* or Naturalist, literary movement and Hakuchō's close involvement with it.

On August 2, 1905, Hakuchō began to address himself for the first time to the problem of devising a theory of fiction in "On reading the *Doppo-shū.*" Mainly of interest is that Hakuchō assesses fiction in terms of its ability to re-create objective reality. In time the aim of the Naturalist writers in Japan would be to re-create such reality in art, even to the point of reliance upon autobiography to insure the verisimilitude and veracity they sought.

Hakuchō immediately followed his praise of Doppo with an article on August 6, 1905, in which he assailed the former literary idol, the great Romantic writer Ozaki Kōyō, claiming that Kōyō lacked the fictional power to portray convincingly the transformation from scholar to usurer of the character Kan'ichi in the perennial favorite *Konjiki yasha* (Gold Demon). September, 1905, saw the long-awaited return of the most influential of the Waseda literati Shimamura Hōgetsu, after a stay of three and a half years in England and Germany. In January, 1906, the periodical *Waseda Bungaku* (Waseda Literature) was revived under the direction of Hōgetsu; in the next few years it would be one of the major vehicles for the products of Japanese literary Naturalism.

In February, 1906, Hakuchō's second story, "Discord and Harmony," appeared. It was an ambitious effort, only partially successful, and only slightly more realistic than his first story had been. In March, 1906, the lengthy realistic "masterpiece" *Hakai* (Broken Commandment) by Shimazaki Tōson appeared; it was at about this time that the term *shizenshugi* suddenly became current. In August, 1906, Hakuchō's third story, "The Second-story Window," was published. It shows a considerable advance in the direction of realism, and may be seen as paving the way for his Naturalist stories to follow. It was the first of his stories to appear in *Waseda Bungaku.*

In the next five months, he published three now mostly forgotten stories that failed to build upon the base of realistic technique he had started in "The Second-story Window." Then, in February, 1907, he published "Dust," the story that is usually said to have established him as a writer of fiction.

"Dust" is his first example of Naturalist writing. Nevertheless, Hakuchō was not totally committed to Naturalistic fiction as yet; indeed it seems he never was just a Naturalist — the Naturalist: "a passive observor, a rigorous compiler of human documents.' "[15] He had too much spiritual curiosity, too much inner philosophical turmoil and fear of life ever to be satisfied with simply reproducing small easily recognizable views of it, like an uninspired portrait photographer.

In 1907, for example, the year of "Dust," Hakuchō also published both "Peace of Mind" in June and "Ghost Picture" in July. "Peace of Mind" deals with problems of faith, doubt, and guilt, all presented within the context of Japanese Christianity. "Ghost Picture" deals with seduction, guilt, and murder.

In August, 1907, Tayama Katai published *Futon* (The Bed), a strictly autobiographical, in places somewhat maudlin, account of the middle-aged novelist's infatuation with a young woman literary disciple. *Futon* put the progress of the Naturalist movement into high gear and firmly established, it is said, the fashion of thinly (if at all) disguised autobiography and confession among a large segment of modern Japanese writers.

Naturalism dominated the literary scene in Japan throughout the remaining years of the Meiji era, that is, until about mid-1912. It was for the most part an approach to fiction championed by writers either from the provinces or connected in some way with Waseda University. Hakuchō was a member of both groups; his fictional star rose with those of the other Naturalists, the much-resented collection of upstarts to whom Ueda Bin referred when he said that literature had fallen into the hands of a group of juvenile delinquents.[16]

Hakuchō was definitely a Meiji Naturalist, but not all of his stories were Naturalistic. The whole picture is revealed only when these stories are viewed within the context of his entire life and thought. The "gloom" that characterized Naturalism and Hakuchō's writing during this period continued throughout his life. The facts of his childhood suggest more basic and profound explanations for the dark cast to his nature than merely the influence of *shizenshugi* or of a late-Meiji social and political disillusionment, as is at times alleged.[17]

It seems that by nature Hakuchō was well suited to the negation and pessimism that were at the heart of Naturalistic philosophy in Japan, but perhaps not so totally suited to its literal-minded realism. We will look more closely at the nature of Japanese Naturalism in Chapter 3. However, although we must never dismiss the impact of Hakuchō's involvement with Naturalism upon his literary philosophy, there is much more to his life and thought than purely stylistic questions.

Were it not for Hakuchō's persistent religious searching — his ceaseless inquiry into the credibility of religious faith in the modern age — he might appear just another realistic writer in our eyes. But such was never the case. There was always friction between his expansive, questioning philosophical spirit and the confines of the Naturalistic style with which he was so closely associated. The true justification for our study lies in the sincerity and complexity of Hakuchō's philosophical quest. Our ultimate purpose must be to suggest the beauty of the purity of such sincerity and complexity.

The philosophy of the Naturalist movement involved a refusal to believe in conventional religions or ideals, a striving for truth and reality, and a compulsive urge to confess. The spirit of this philosophy seems illustrated by the marriage of Masamune Hakuchō. In April, 1911, at the age of thirty-two, Hakuchō married Tsune, who was thirteen years younger than he. Hakuchō had been in no hurry to marry at first, but he grew tired of carousing and finally decided it was time. His wedding announcement to his family was a simple card, which did not tell his family anything about the girl, her age, how he met her, or about the girl's family.

Three months after the wedding, in July, 1911, the story "Clay Doll" appeared in the *Waseda Bungaku*. Hakuchō himself later said that he rushed into marriage blindly in an attempt to put some emotional order back into his muddled life, but he found that traces of his muddled life remained with him even after his marriage.

The frankly autobiographical "Clay Doll" is for the most part, as Hakuchō admitted, an accurate account of his wedding experiences.[18] The hero of the story, Jūkichi, finds his virginal young wife, Tokiko, to be boring and insufferable. He spends the first week of their marriage out on the town every night looking for some diversion, while his despairing wife waits at home in sorrow and confusion.

In "Clay Doll" Tokiko turns more and more to Buddhism for consolation, whereas Jūkichi is never able to accept the ordinary, rather slow-witted but harmless girl as the wife for whom he had waited all his life. He considers her a doll, a lifeless, meaningless object. Nevertheless, Hakuchō and his wife had a long and happy life together. He became famous for his affection for his wife; he was habitually kind to her.

Perhaps Tsune influenced and mellowed Hakuchō over the years. In 1964 Mrs. Masamune said that his attitude toward her when they were first married was exactly as it is exhibited in "Clay Doll," although she was not too clear in 1964 whether he actually stayed out at night the first week. Even if he had, she saw nothing so strange in that, for she found such behavior characteristic of young men. She was quite assured that the reason the story impressed its readers was that it was so factual.[19] Be that as it may, there were many critics who complained of the bad aftertaste the story left and its general unpleasantness.

Tsune described Hakuchō as adrift at the time of their marriage;[20] his marriage helped to anchor him somewhat. His string of fictional successes — "Wasted Effort" (1910), "Faint Light" (1910), and "Clay Doll" — brought him financial and emotional stability.

V *Beyond Naturalism*

Hakuchō's first play, *White Wall,* appeared in April, 1912. In all, Hakuchō wrote forty plays, most of them between February, 1924, and May, 1928. Hakuchō had long admired *kabuki* plays, in particular the works of Kawatake Mokuami, for their poetic beauty and the charm of their Edo emotionalism. However, Hakuchō's plays, although not totally without traces of *kabuki* influence, were thoroughly modern in form and spirit.

Writing plays was one way that Hakuchō sought to respond to the changing literary scene as Naturalism became passé. *White*

Wall was modelled on the lives of his father and grandfather. It differs considerably in mood and conception from Hakuchō's fiction of the years 1907 through 1911.

Another role Hakuchō adopted in the wake of the age of Naturalism was that of newspaper novelist,[21] but this was to be a far less satisfying one than that of playwright. He had written his first serial in 1909, and this was followed by another which appeared in 1911–1912. Hakuchō did not like writing for newspapers, for he felt that the demands of pure literature were incompatible with the transient nature of newspaper writing where something is written one day and forgotten the next.[22]

Hakuchō serialized five more novels in newspapers from 1912 through 1919. After the discouraging halt to one of these, because of a lack of reader response, he was forced to produce manuscripts at a rapid pace. He wrote twenty stories in 1913 and 1914, in addition to the play *The Secret* (August, 1914).

His next significant work, however, was the story "By the Inlet" which appeared in April, 1915. It is a thinly disguised autobiography set in his home town. The memorable character is the hero's younger brother, a solitary, friendless fellow whom the hero — who is somewhat of a success in Tokyo — feels he might even have come to resemble had he stayed home.

"The Smell of the Cowshed" (May, 1916) is another story set in Honami. It is an effective fictionalization of an unfortunate, impoverished family that lived for generations in a shed near the Masamune family home.

Hakuchō wrote little of interest for nearly five years, as he entered a period of literary silence. From 1916 through 1920 Hakuchō thought frequently of giving up literature. From 1915 to 1917 he was troubled by a variety of stomach ailments which added to his weariness. However, the source of his dissatisfaction with literature was his concept of literature, which was still dominated by an image of the role of the writer, a concept shaped largely by Hakuchō's experiences with Japanese Naturalism.

In seeking veracity in their writing, Japanese Naturalists had turned to their own real-life experience for material. They simply offered their lives to their readers, piece by piece, fact by fact, as Hakuchō himself had done in "Clay Doll." Many of these writers, especially Chikamatsu Shūkō and Tokuda Shūsei, were promiscuous and somewhat Bohemian, so that their fiction was often simply accounts of their affairs with geisha.

Such Naturalist writers maintained a steady output of stories to finance their lives, which included such expensive amusements as geisha. They often sought adventures and involvement with prostitutes to supply unusual incidents for their fiction, the sale of which financed further forays into the demimonde, and so on.

Hakuchō exhausted his well of inspiration for such stories with "Faint Light" and "Attempted Double Suicide" (1913). He had begun to frequent brothels in his newspaper days, but he now began to stop such diversions. He began to feel that his life was sordid and he went alternately to the mountains and the sea in an effort to break the spell of his unsatisfying style of life.

Through his involvement with the Naturalist literary movement, Hakuchō had allowed himself to become preoccupied with the ephemera of literature. He had been so busy living up to his image of literary figure that he had lost touch with the philosophical core of literature. He had abandoned his former habits of copious reading and religious speculation. "Fame" had distracted him from the Bible, Homer, Dante, and Tolstoy — all that had led him to literature in the first place. The result was restlessness and frustration.

In mid-November, 1919, Hakuchō gave up his house in Tokyo and returned to his home town of Honami. Hakuchō had always felt that if his ability or desire to write stories ever deserted him, he could "retire" to his home town to spend the rest of his days. He was not happy at home, however. At first, since he was now "famous," he was looked up to by his many younger brothers and sisters. However, he soon came to find it humiliating to live there idly, and felt that he was in effect a nuisance to his relatives. By May, 1920, he wanted to return to Tokyo.

When he returned to Tokyo, he was unable to find a suitable house to rent. From the summer of 1920 to the spring of 1921 Hakuchō continued his migrations, ostensibly in search of a house, but in fact in search of a retreat, that is, a sanctuary at which he could put some psychological and philosophical order back into his life. After Tokyo he lived briefly in Ikaho, Karuizawa, Tokyo again, two locations in the little town of Ōiso where he had gone on the recommendation of a friend, his wife's place in Kōfu, Tokyo a third time, and finally back to Ōiso.

VI   *At Ōiso*

This time Hakuchō and his wife were to stay in Ōiso for twelve years, before moving back to Tokyo in 1933. His recent experiences had completely dispelled his long-cherished fantasy that he could return to the womb of his home town any time things became too difficult to manage in Tokyo. He now set to work, once settled, writing more diligently than ever before.

With "Various People" (September, 1921) Hakuchō evolved a new literary style to replace, partially at least, the outmoded Naturalism. This new style involved the expression of his views of life and humanity in the context of a fictional narrative based upon material taken from his own experiences and surroundings. These new stories were in effect philosophical autobiographical sketches.

Hakuchō's final move to Ōiso was an important one for his writing and philosophy. In Ōiso Hakuchō had solitude for the first time and was able to concentrate on his studies and on the writing of plays, criticism, and essays. The move to Ōiso brought about a return of his interest in extensive reading. He resumed his reading but not his Christian faith, although he did begin to treat essentially religious matters usually from the point of view of the skeptic, which culminated in such works as "On Dante" (1927) and "Uchimura Kanzō" (1949).

In Ōiso Hakuchō found an environment which, free of the distractions of his relatives in Honami and the literary scene in Tokyo, afforded the calm needed to turn his thoughts inward to achieve further depth in his writings. His writings turned from mere descriptions of objective phenomena — although they were perhaps seldom "merely" that — to description that tried to point to the philosophical significance that might lie behind such objective reality. A new depth and seriousness of purpose is reflected in the plays, stories, and essays of Hakuchō's "Ōiso period." Now possible was such fiction as the highly imaginative story "Illusion" which appeared in May, 1922, and which owes some of its symbolic language to Dante's *Divine Comedy*.

The period of Hakuchō's greatest activity as a playwright began in 1924. At the same time, he emerged as a leading literary critic about 1926 through his regular column, "Timely Critique of Literature," in which he discussed briefly a few new works that caught his notice and then proceeded to comment critically on any writing that interested him. The twelve "Timely Critique" columns he contributed to twelve consecutive issues of the *Chūō Kōron,* those of January through December, 1926, fostered debate as his opinions of various works and writers called forth rebuttals from such writers as Nagai Kafu.[23]

From 1924 through 1927 Hakuchō was engaged in the writing of plays and criticism, but he also wrote several stories. The most important of these was the lengthy "I Killed a Man, And Yet," which was serialized from June 21, 1925, to September 27, 1925. It is an unusual story, containing several murders. It was, for Hakuchō, a long work, which he composed with excruciating effort and concentration only to have it criticized as a work of pure fancy totally lacking in — ironically — realism.[24]

From November 23, 1928, to December 21, 1929, Hakuchō and Tsune were away from Japan on a fruitful but exhausting tour of Hawaii, the United States, France, England, Italy, Switzerland, and Germany. The literary scene in Japan changed while Hakuchō was away in Europe; interest in the leftist literature of the Proletarian Literary Movement was then at its height. It was a time of increasing involvement of men of letters in political activity.

Many writers risked their lives through association with the outlawed Communist Party. Others were attracted to the legal left-wing parties, such as the Social Democratic Party. It differed from such illegal parties as the Communist Party in that, unlike the latter, it supported the "emperor system" (*tennōsei*).[25] In this period of general political polarization and increasing politicization of literature, the social democratic philosophy attracted many intellectuals, including writers.

Writers even ran for public office. Kikuchi Kan was a candidate of the Social Democrats in the Tokyo municipal elections in 1927 and again in the elections for representatives to the Diet in 1928. Kagawa Toyohiko was a candidate of the Social Democrats for the Diet from Tokyo in 1930.[26] An indication of the pervasiveness of this trend toward involvement of literary figures in politics is the fact that, for a time in February, 1930, even the archetypical patron of geisha and Naturalist writer Tokuda Shūsei seriously considered candidacy for a seat in the Diet's Lower House.

A strong impulse to withdraw always existed in Hakuchō. This was something both psychological, a personality trait, and philosophical, that is, an intellectual stance which attracted him. In Chapter 5, we shall examine at length the implications, in this light, of Hakuchō's essay "On Dante," which was written in 1927 when the intrusion of political thought into literature was gathering momentum.

"On Dante" is a cry for solitude. It is an elegy to the religious fervor of the Middle Ages of Europe and Japan. Although it is a literary essay, rather than a philosophical manifesto, it may be taken as a rejection of exclusive preoccupation with objective, purely phenomenal reality. In a sense, then, it is a rejection of his earlier Naturalistic philosophical stance, which was predicated upon the primacy of such reality.

Although he recognized the importance of political disappointment in shaping the life and art of Dante, Hakuchō was drawn to the image of Dante in exile, looking upon the injustice of the world of men with sad disgust. "On Dante" is certainly not the work of a man inclined to puzzle over the ideologies of transitory political parties. Such a stance set him quietly at odds with the mood of the times, however. As a result, publishers ceased to be interested in the basically apolitical Hakuchō during those years. In 1930 he contented himself with travel sketches based upon his recent journey.

From January to April, 1931, he serialized "The Caller Didn't Come," which was flawed by a needlessly slow-paced narrative.[27] He remained active as a critic in 1931 and 1932; in 1932 he also wrote two plays. In 1933 and 1934, rather than fiction he relied upon sketches of authors and contemporary criticism.

VII   *The 1930s and the War*

In 1933 Hakuchō left Ōiso and moved to Tokyo; in April, 1934, his father died in Honami. Hakuchō went to his father's bedside, and he turned his sad experience into the short story "Spring This Year" (June, 1934). In it we see his mother worn from nursing her husband during his illness of some eleven years; Hakuchō is forced to watch his father linger in increasing pain for over twenty days. The onslaught of his father's infirmities in 1923 had been the occasion for Hakuchō's receipt of one-third of the family property; with his father's death Hakuchō inherited the headship of the Masamune family.

In June and July, 1935, Hakuchō and his wife toured Hokkaido and Sakhalin. Having returned from this trip, the Masamunes soon set out again for Seoul, Mukden, Hsinking (the capital of Manchukuo), and Peking. Hakuchō had never had a great interest in the Chinese civilization and there were few places he especially wanted to visit. Little that he saw impressed him, although some spots near Peking moved him, not the architecture itself, but the thought that men could raise such buildings in the midst of that great plain. Nonetheless, his account of his journey to China wears a bored, melancholy air.[28]

In the 1930s Hakuchō was more important as a literary critic than as a writer of fiction or as a playwright. With the changing literary scene discouraging him as a novelist, he settled naturally and comfortably into the role of literary critic. Well known in his lively debate with the critic Kobayashi Hideo in the first half of 1936, the so-called "thought and real life" (*shisō to jisseikatsu*) debate.

The debate was occasioned by Kobayashi's objection to Hakuchō's biographical approach to his interpretation of the works of Tolstoy in "On Tolstoy." Kobayashi argued against the need to look for the origins of Tolstoy's philosophy in the facts of his life. For, Kobayashi reasoned, ultimately the "thought" a man spawns takes on a separate and independent existence from that of its creator. Throughout, however, Hakuchō maintained that "thought" — the abstract — cannot come into existence without "real life" — the concrete. Since the concrete precedes the abstract, the origins of the abstract may be sought in the concrete. Study of the "real life" origins of abstract "thought" can be one way of better understanding the latter, Hakuchō explained.

Hakuchō and his wife embarked on their second trip to the West in July, 1936, touring Russia, Northern Europe, France, Germany, and the United States, before returning in February, 1937. Hakuchō was again restless, having made trips to Sakhalin, Korea, and China, and now a second voyage around the world. With the inheritance of his considerable family fortune and his interest in such time-consuming amusements as golf, Hakuchō seemed to lose much of his creative energy.

In 1937 the political situation in Japan would continue to worsen until it affected every facet of Japanese life. The fighting began with the incident between Japanese and Chinese troops at the Marco Polo Bridge near Peking on the night of July 7, 1937, and led to destruction, defeat, and atomic holocaust eight years later in the summer of 1945. Hakuchō's career followed a similar downward course, as his output of fiction and criticism began to decline in 1937 and decreased annually to the point where he produced next to nothing from 1943 through 1945.

Hakuchō engaged in what literary activity was permitted by the government in the early 1940s, but it was of the most sterile form, that of literary meetings and speech-making rather than literary publication. In 1937, however, men of letters still had the freedom, short-lived though it proved to be, to refuse to participate in government-controlled literary organizations. Hakuchō was one of the many who declined appointment to the government's Teikoku Geijutsuin (Imperial Academy of Art). Hakuchō declined in June, 1937; he did not become a member until urged to reconsider in August, 1940.[29]

During the war Hakuchō restricted himself to activity in literary organizations. With the deaths of Shūsei and Tōson in 1943 and Shūkō in 1944, Hakuchō became a grand old man of letters, being in his mid-sixties during World War II. Thus it is little surprise that he was made president of the Japan P.E.N. Club in 1943 and the head of the Nihon Bungaku Hōkokukai (Japan Patriotic Literature Society) in 1944. He had been named a director of the Kokumin Geijutsu Gikai (National Arts Council) in February, 1940.

In January, 1942, Hakuchō began serialization of the long work "Duckweed," although it was discontinued after eight months. It is a story based upon his memory of his childhood and adolescence.

From the late Taishō period Hakuchō often summered in Karuizawa. From August, 1944, as the war situation deteriorated, Hakuchō lived in Karuizawa, not as a man summering in a villa but as a member of a neighborhood association taking part in air-raid drills and doing farm labor. His wife and his young nephew Yūzō, whom he had adopted, bicycled about taking care of the food-hunting chores. Hakuchō did the housekeeping and cooked for himself and for about one year had no opportunity to write. The life to which the militarists had led the Japanese in the last year of the war allowed no time for art; there was only survival.

Hakuchō was safe physically during his evacuation to Karuizawa, but he lost his home and property in Tokyo to incendiary bombs on May 25, 1945. The war made Hakuchō feel his isolation as an individual, that is, feel that he was unique as a human being ultimately in spite of the superficial resemblances all men share.[30] The war made Hakuchō keenly aware of the mood of alienation from society and his fellow man, the wall of noncommunication, that began to characterize Japanese fiction more than at any period in the past.

VIII   Postwar Literary Activity

Hakuchō entered a new period of intense literary activity in the late 1940s. He hit his writing peak in 1949 and 1950 at ages seventy and seventy-one. He described his wartime existence in Karuizawa as having been "hell,"[31] but with the new freedom to publish which peace brought he flourished. He produced many essays in the 1940s and 1950s, delving into his relationship with literature and the effect of it upon his life and psychology. Among these is his "History of the Rise and Fall of Naturalist Literature" (1948), a long, insider's view of the late Meiji *shizenshugi bungaku* (Naturalist literature) movement.

In 1949 he produced several notable works. These include: "The Misanthrope" (January through June), "Uchimura Kanzō" (April and May), and "Escape from Japan" (begun in January, added to periodically, but left incomplete after March, 1953). "The Misanthrope" is an episodic account of his lonely life as an evacuee in the last days of the war and its devastating effect upon him. "Uchimura Kanzō" is a passionate description of the influence of Uchimura upon Hakuchō, in which he relies upon biographies of Uchimura, his own memories, Uchimura's complete works, and, of course, the Bible (in particular Paul's Epistle to the Romans). It is clear from his discussion of Uchimura that Hakuchō is still unable to accept certain of Christianity's doctrines, such as that of the Second Coming. Nevertheless, as in many earlier works, Hakuchō expresses his envy of those possessed of absolute faith.

"Escape from Japan" is Hakuchō's longest postwar work, a "fairy tale" (*otogi-banashi*), that owes much of its fantastic language and imagery to such sources as Bakin's *Hakkenden, The Iliad,* Dante's *Divine Comedy,* Boccaccio's *Decameron,* Jonathan Swift, and August Strindberg. Its fanciful language shows, if nothing else, that Hakuchō was not just a realistic writer in the manner of, say, Tokuda Shūsei. Despite its unusual style and importance as a key to Hakuchō's psychology, it got out of Hakuchō's control and he was forced to leave it uncompleted.

During the 1940s Hakuchō was becoming distressed with the direction Japanese fiction was taking. Specifically, he deplored the rampant eroticism and what he took to be a lack of self-examination in fiction. He had had high hopes for postwar fiction, but he felt his expectations had been too optimistic. Hakuchō felt even the small literary periodicals were pandering to the low standard of public taste and scurrying to publish whatever would sell.

Hakuchō was undergoing a major change in his attitude toward literature at this time. He no longer felt that the re-creation of objective reality was the highest purpose of fiction. He now

believed that such strict adherence to reality would lead literature to
a creative impasse. He had begun to feel the need to abandon
entirely the Naturalistic approach. Hakuchō now wanted to make
the world of fantasy his world.[32]

IX Disillusionment with Literature

In the 1950s Hakuchō realized that philosophical speculation was
his central concern and that art functioned primarily as a tool for
understanding the nature of his existence. He felt the experience of
the war had created a new consciousness. He considered the war an
experience whose psychological horror and philosophical impact
were unimaginable to those who had not actually lived through it.

Given Hakuchō's constant awareness and fear of death, his terror of the war must have been intense. He even declared such prewar writers as Sōseki, Ōgai, and Tōson mediocre because of what
he came to regard as the superficiality of their perception of reality.
He felt that they had never had to reexamine their conception of
reality the way those who lived through the entire experience of the
war did.

Hakuchō's observation is understandable, perhaps, in the sense
that with the defeat every Japanese must have had to reassess the
implications of his Japaneseness, whereas those Japanese, writers
as well as average citizens, who never knew defeat were spared such
self-examination. However, it is difficult to agree with the implication that prewar and postwar experience was fundamentally different on the existential level, for no man is spared a knowledge of
pain, fear, and death, certainly not the three giants of Meiji literature that Hakuchō mentions. Such extreme pronouncements can
perhaps be regarded as symptomatic of Hakuchō's growing disenchantment with literature.

Hakuchō expected a revolution of sorts from postwar Japanese
literature,[33] but the new literature he hoped for never materialized.
He simply became more disenchanted. In March, 1957, a collection
of his essays, *Doubt and Belief,* appeared which contained pieces
from as early as September, 1953, and as recent as January, 1957.
The bulk of his essays, however, are from the year 1956. This was a
period of worldwide concern over the dangers of the atomic bomb
and the threat of a third world war between the communist world
and the so-called free world. It was also a time marked by considerable public reaction to the alleged moral dangers posed by such

recent works of literature as Ishihara Shintarō's novel of rebellious youth, *Taiyō no kisetsu* (Season of Violence) (1955), and Tanizaki Jun'ichirō's novel of middle-aged sexual adventure, *Kagi* (The Key) (1956).

Many of the essays comprising *Doubt and Belief* are topical yet read quite well even now. Hakuchō's concern ranges from such eternal matters as art and religion to current phenomena such as Billy Graham, the new religions of Japan, eroticism in fiction, white prejudices against nonwhites, debates over capital punishment, and, above all, nuclear weapons. The cloud of the atomic bomb casts its shadow over much of his thought in *Doubt and Belief*.

Oiwa Kō, who was a friend of Hakuchō from the 1940s and who last saw him in the fall of 1961, a year before his death, notes that from 1957–1958 Hakuchō began to speak often of death.[34] Oiwa sees Hakuchō as preparing for the eventual profession of his Christian faith by writing the various essays concerned with religious questions that are contained in the two volumes *Autumn of This Year* (May, 1959), which won the Yomiuri Prize for Literature in 1960, and *One Secret* (November, 1961). The story "Autumn of This Year," an autobiographical account of the recent death of his brother, had appeared in January, 1959.

In "Autumn of This Year" Hakuchō speaks of the blessings of baptism. The question that tormented Hakuchō in "Autumn of This Year" was whether he would call upon Christ when he himself was about to die. *One Secret* exhibits admiration for Christianity and envy of the solace faith can give one at death.

On the night of April 12, 1962, Hakuchō gave a speech, "Sixty Years of Literary Life," which appeared in the *Chūō Kōron* in December, 1962. He said he had reached no conclusions about the nature of human existence, that no matter how long he lived he could get no satisfactory answers to the problem of existence. Even in the novels of Tolstoy and Dostoyevsky he could not find what he was seeking; literature was only momentary consolation. He felt his life and work amounted to nothing; he had tried to resign himself to those facts, but somehow he could not fully.

He said that he felt grateful for the life of Christ, and found His coming to earth as an ordinary mortal especially noble. But Hakuchō wondered why he could not be blessed with the miracle of faith and lose his anguish through its consolation. Hakuchō felt that his art was doomed to despair. Although he realized that one might win praise for one's literature of despair, he also wondered why no one wrote a literature of faith. In concluding "Sixty Years of Literary Life," he speculated whether man with his limited powers can hope to attain that wonderful something for which he is destined in life; Hakuchō confessed that he was constantly beset by that question — can man hope for spiritual peace?

X The Death of Hakuchō

In the summer of 1961, the year before he died, Hakuchō told a friend that he wanted a Buddhist funeral. On March 29, 1962, he told the Reverend Uemura Tamaki, the daughter of his former pastor Uemura Masahisa, that he would like a Christian funeral.

Hakuchō was aware that he had no religion of his own, so that on April 1, 1962, he visited Uemura Tamaki to ask her to conduct his funeral. She hesitated to commit herself to a definite promise, however, for she wanted to affirm Hakuchō's faith in Christianity.[35]

On April 18 Uemura visited Hakuchō's home and held Christian services there. Listening to her sing hymns that her father had loved, Hakuchō may have thought of her father and felt as if she were telling him through her actions that she would agree to conduct his funeral after all.[36] There were a number of participants in the prayer meeting besides the Masamunes and Uemura. Because of this, there was no opportunity to discuss Hakuchō's funeral arrangements. No definite agreement was made between Uemura and Hakuchō, but it seems as if there was an unspoken one.

Hakuchō seemed to be acting upon this unspoken agreement which he felt he had with Uemura for he became more of a Christian in the orthodox sense. In mid-May he attended services at a Christian church in Tokyo, perhaps because he wished to have his funeral held there;[37] in August he visited a Christian church in Karuizawa.

In the summer of 1962 Hakuchō's health deteriorated rapidly so that in early August he went to Karuizawa to remove himself from the stifling heat of Tokyo, which was making his stomach pains increasingly acute. About August 20 there were signs that his condition had suddenly taken another turn for the worse; on August 25 he returned to Tokyo for treatment. He weighed less than eighty pounds when he entered the hospital; exploratory surgery on September 5 revealed cancer of the pancreas.

After the operation Hakuchō's appetite returned and he relaxed by reading Gibbon's *The Rise and Fall of the Roman Empire,* but about September 20 he lost his appetite again. According to his wife Tsune's "Byōshō nisshi" (Daily Report by a Sickbed) (January, 1963), Hakuchō told her on October 6 to have Uemura preside over his funeral, a simple funeral with just a few relatives present. On October 11, Tsune visited Uemura and asked for her help should the worst come and she readily agreed.

On October 12, Uemura began her daily visits to Hakuchō's hospital room, where she sang hymns and prayed. On one occasion, his wife reports, he grasped Uemura's arm firmly and looked up at her in gratitude. The entry of Tsune's "Byōshō nisshi" for October 16, 1962, states that Hakuchō had told her he was not a large (*tairyō aru*) enough person to abandon everything and follow Christ. Yet on October 25, Hakuchō said that he wanted his funeral held in a church.

Hakuchō died on the morning of October 28, 1962; Uemura Tamaki's account of his last hours appeared on October 29. She had asked Hakuchō if he believed in Christ. His reply was broken, but he said that he had done many wrong things, but since Christ had forgiven him, he could go to Christ's side (*mimoto*).

When Uemura had finished praying by his bedside, Hakuchō clearly added "Amen," which would indicate that he was participating in the prayer. Given Hakuchō's familiarity with the Bible and Christianity it can be assumed that he understood the Christian use of the word "amen" to indicate agreement with what has been said, usually the content of some form of prayer.

Hakuchō asked to have a simple funeral and confessed that he had been unkind to many people in his lifetime and wanted to apologize to those he had wronged. His desire to reconcile himself with everyone before dying, to leave this world with his ledger clean, is an attitude which although not exclusively Christian is nevertheless central in Christian thinking. The Christian must leave this world without sin, he must have repented and forgiven his transgressors. This is an attitude of humility which the Christian seeks in emulation of the example of Jesus who willingly died on the cross and asked God's forgiveness for his murderers.

Tsune's "Daily Report by a Sickbed" shows that Hakuchō was weak, frightened, and confused during his last weeks. Death from pancreatic cancer was certain, and he perceived that despite her attempts to reassure him. His death was prolonged and painful.

Something sustained him, however. The noted surgeon who attended him had never read any of his works. In his own account of Hakuchō's death, he notes that when he and the hospital staff got their first look at their famous patient, they were at a loss to discover any possible source of Hakuchō's "greatness." After Hakuchō's death, however, the doctor wrote that Hakuchō's corpse inspired feelings of "serenity itself" (*heisei sono mono*) like few he had seen.[38]

Uemura recounts how Hakuchō took her hand and told her how Kunikida Doppo, when he was dying, had called for her father and told him to pray, lamenting that he himself could not pray. (In 1954 Hakuchō had written that, like Doppo, he too would probably be unable to pray when his time came.)[39] As Hakuchō held her hand and gazed steadily at her, she felt he was emphasizing that he had indeed been able to join her in prayer through his "Amen." She was moved to the point of tears.[40]

Uemura notes that at the end Hakuchō became like a child. She asked him to believe wholeheartedly in Christ, to accept the fact that He died on the cross for man's sins, and to follow his Lord meekly. She says that to this Hakuchō replied clearly, "I now believe wholeheartedly; I will obey [Christ]."[41]

In the light of Hakuchō's activities and attitudes during 1962 it is difficult to account for the tremendous reaction to Uemura Tamaki's revelation of Hakuchō's Christian faith. The whole furor that followed — thirty articles appearing in four months — is an indication of the stature of Hakuchō in the minds of his literary colleagues. It is customary to eulogize a departed writer widely in Japan, but rarely does a novelist die a natural death, as opposed to suicide, and cause a sensation. Although some felt compelled to assert that Hakuchō never returned to the faith, most of the debate was over the exact time Hakuchō returned to Christianity and not a dispute over whether he did indeed die a Christian.

Some of the more extreme interpretations of Hakuchō's death can be discounted. For example, there is no indication of any brain impairment in Tsune's "Byōshō nisshi" from the time Hakuchō entered the hospital until his death. Until there is evidence of a conspiracy to pass the dying atheist Hakuchō off to the world as a Christian, the accounts of Tsune and Uemura Tamaki will have to be trusted.

CHAPTER 2

The Early Stories

I N examining the fiction of Masamune Hakuchō, two aspects
concern us. First are stylistic considerations, such as the presence or absence of realism and the thematic structure of his works.
As we saw, he first achieved notice as a Naturalistic writer. His earliest stories reveal that he had from the beginning much of what
would later be called a Naturalistic outlook. Also, although Japanese commentators often confine their stylistic discussions to questions of literary schools and "isms," a brief examination of the
structure of his stories (see Chapter 4, VI) should be of use in high-
lighting the recurrent patterns of Hakuchō's artistic imagination.

Our second concern is philosophical content. Hakuchō is seldom
thought of as a stylist. He was a literary philosopher; at least that is
his primary importance to Japanese students of his writing today,
fifteen years after his death. He was as literary as philosophical,
however. If we expect tightly reasoned logic from him, he will dis-
appoint us. His philosophical points at times fail to lead to a firm
conclusion. His stories often end on a note of ambiguity. If we
think of his life — the trail of his personal philosophy — the philosophical ambiguity of some of his fiction seems understandable.
Above all, we must note his attitude toward Christianity, wherever
it reveals itself.

I *"Solitude" (1904)*

Kobayashi Hideo, who was well acquainted with both Hakuchō
and his writings, was one critic who classified Hakuchō as a religious writer,[1] and quite justifiably. For a religious element can be
seen throughout the career of Hakuchō; it asserts itself to different
degrees in different periods of his life but finally emerges as the
essence of his thought and art.

Hakuchō's first story, "Solitude," concerns aspiring young

39

painters. The protagonist is Sawatani, who has devoted himself to his painting for years with little recognition. He often involves himself so single-mindedly in his painting that he forgets to eat or is oblivious to the winter cold.

"Solitude" opens with a description of a sketch of Sawatani's masterpiece, a painting entitled "The Conscript," in which a church with a cross looms in the distance behind the conscript. Gotō finds this church with its cross quite portentous, for he feels the church and cross are in the background not only of the painting in "Solitude" but of all of Hakuchō's works as well.[2]

Hakuchō was always concerned with the fundamental questions of the nature and meaning of his existence. Because of his early religious training, he would generally probe these questions within a Christian context. This set him off from his less philosophical or less Christian colleagues. It is indeed of significance that Christian symbols appear even in his first work of fiction.

The habits of the serious young painter Sawatani are contrasted with those of his hedonistic and carefree fellow painter, Yumoto. Sawatani's rival Yumoto has a reputation for his way with women as well as for his painting skill.

Fame suddenly comes to Sawatani through an exhibition of works by young artists. Sawatani has gone to the gallery only out of a sense of duty; he fully expects to be seared by the judges. He is startled to find a wealthy patron — a judge of the contest — standing before his painting extolling its genius to the passing crowds. The timid, unkempt Sawatani finds the courage to identify himself as the painter.

The wealthy patron's beautiful daughter is also present; she looks Sawatani in the eye and declares his work superior to the much-ballyhooed painting by Yumoto. Sawatani is electrified; the eyes of all the spectators are upon them — the genius and the beauty. Could that dishevelled young man have painted that masterpiece, they wonder. Sawatani is now aglow as they move off to the lounge: the old man asking many questions and holding a cigar; the young girl "more beautiful than any in the paintings"; and the artist losing all track of time as he eagerly expounds his theories of art.

Hakuchō's immaturity is evident from the grandness and theatricality of this scene. We wonder whether he thinks he is being somehow Tolstoyean or if this is the provincial Hakuchō's wide-eyed conception of "Art" and "Culture." Hakuchō's attitude toward his material makes it difficult to speak of "Solitude" in terms of Naturalistic fiction.

Meanwhile, Yumoto, who himself had earlier had fame and the support of this art patron sees his reputation suffer. In the end, the unscrupulous Yumoto talks the beautiful daughter — who is in love with him — into lending him some money before he sails off to America.

Sawatani is unhappy, despite his new fame and fortune. He has lost his motivation to paint, because the realization of what had been his dream — recognition — has brought him not pleasure, but loneliness. He is disillusioned; the solitude he had enjoyed as an aspiring painter now brings him feelings of emptiness. Although Yumoto seems to envy Sawatani his success, Sawatani strongly envies Yumoto his pleasures. Yumoto is publicly disgraced because of his affairs, but Sawatani thinks they must bring more happiness than his own superficial fame.

Hakuchō's postscript states that both young men leave Japan on the same ship for the West. The one, we know, is going off to study, bearing the hopes of the artistic community, whereas the other is sneaking off to atone for his disgrace. "On which should we pin our hopes?"[3] concludes Hakuchō. Who is happier after all: the man with fame and respectability or the man who follows his passions though they lead him to disgrace?

The problem of leisure which appears here was a familiar theme in Hakuchō's fiction. Sawatani's spiritual "torment" derives largely from success, wealth, and free time. Hakuchō is not specific in identifying this problem, but most of his anguished young men seem to have limitless amounts of free time. Despite such notable exceptions as "Dust" (1907) and "The Smell of the Cowshed" (1916), there is seldom the feeling of problems compounded by pressing obligations, such as the need to work. Hakuchō's literature is a literature of leisure; his characters generally have all the time they need to sit and brood, thrash aimlessly about the streets of Tokyo, and run off to the country for a change of scenery or mood.

Hakuchō's idea of what constitutes culture or art can perhaps be detected. Art is high art: it is classical or Western; it is certainly not folk or rural in any way. The irony in this is that Hakuchō's characters are often like himself; they are provincials who have come to the capital and adopted its values. They cannot be at home in the provinces anymore; they are rustics who are only at home in the city. These values seem to determine the success of "Solitude." Although the events of the story are believable, in the sense of being possible, they are presented through immature eyes. The effectiveness of the story is damaged when Hakuchō becomes artificially theatrical. "Solitude" is the first of many depictions of lonely young men, but only a preliminary sketch, not a finished portrait.

II   *"Discord and Harmony" (1906) and*
"The Second-story Window" (1906)

Hakuchō's second story, "Discord and Harmony," appeared about six months after he became convinced that he could write like Doppo. In that story the handsome young hero hears that the woman he has always loved, who has returned from an unsuccessful marriage, is immoral. This leads him to go ahead and marry the homely daughter of a rich family, whom his parents had encouraged him to marry. He soon becomes addicted to his family routine and "a slave to his abacus and his account book."[4] His first love is left alone and bitter.

Despite the title and some of Hakuchō's comments on his hero's situation, however, to Ōiwa Kō this second story is without the striking revelations of life's sad and seamy side that would mark Hakuchō's Naturalistic fiction.[5] What ties there are with his later works seem significant, nonetheless. The irresolute character of the hero, Kiyoshi, calls to mind that of a later Hakuchō hero, Suganuma Kenji of "Whither?"; the helplessness of even such a strong female character as O-Suma, the woman Kiyoshi loves who was supposedly an adulteress, is repeated in that of the heroines of "Faint Light" and "Clay Doll."

"Discord and Harmony" projects a feeling of inevitability, which is expressed in traditionally fatalistic terms, rather than in terms of the scientific determinism commonly associated with Naturalism, especially in the West. Kiyoshi is being pressured to marry the rich girl in order to save his mother and younger sister from the insurmountable debts accumulated by his irresponsible late father. Kobayashi, the father of the rich girl, is their creditor; Kiyoshi's old-fashioned uncle is always reminding Kiyoshi of his duty to his mother, his sister, the name of his dead father, and even to Kobayashi, who had helped finance Kiyoshi's education. When he declares his love to the divorced O-Suma, however, she encourages him to have strength and to face the abuse of their relatives and society together with her. They are on the point of escaping to start a new life together, when a meddlesome but well-meaning friend tells Kiyoshi that adultery was the cause of her divorce.

Kiyoshi had known that her husband was a thoroughly despicable person, and also that there was some suspicion about her and her handsome brother-in-law, but he had never believed the worst. She herself had been evasive about the reason for her divorce, but she had warned Kiyoshi of the recklessness of his meddlesome friend. We could then also interpret events as the friend slandering O-Suma, whose relations with her brother-in-law may have been innocent after all.

Kiyoshi receives a letter from O-Suma saying that she will hate him for the rest of her life because he believed his friend rather than her. Thereupon, Hakuchō sums things up very quickly in a manner and tone which will be repeated in such later stories as "Dust" and "Clay Doll." Hakuchō notes that Kiyoshi has become a slave of middle-class routine — he leaves for work at eight each morning and returns each day at four; O-Suma, Kiyoshi has heard, has become the mistress of a certain gentleman. Kiyoshi assumes she lives in sorrow, reviling the cruel world.

What limits the success of "Discord and Harmony" to some extent is the first-person point of view, which seems to restrict the narrative flow. Since it is the story of O-Suma as well as of Kiyoshi, it might have been told more easily by an omniscient third-person narrator. Hakuchō also includes scenes featuring Kiyoshi's uncle, mother, and sister, as well as many which develop the character of his meddlesome friend. It is a long story, forty-two pages as it appeared in *Shinshōsetsu,* but it does develop and maintain a light hold upon the reader's interest.

The strong-willed beauty O-Suma is fascinating and we are never certain until the next-to-last page whether Kiyoshi will have the sense to throw caution to the wind and run off with her. (Were this a later Hakuchō story, we would not entertain such hopes and would expect a characteristically gloomy ending.)

"Discord and Harmony" contains many descriptions of street scenes and of nature that are somewhat ornate and more typical of earlier fiction than the Naturalism that was to come. It is not until "Dust" that Hakuchō evolves an economical, direct style, free of such digressions. Likewise, it is in "Dust" that he creates his most successful first-person story, a tight work focusing on just two characters.

Hakuchō's third story, "The Second-story Window," appeared in *Waseda Bungaku* in August, 1906. It contains a scene in which one character tells another that one cannot find reality depicted in the works of Sir Walter Scott, that one must turn to the works of the *shizen-ha,* or "nature school," for that. Ōiwa notes that it is impossible to tell whether Hakuchō was referring to Naturalism in the sense of *shizenshugi* literature, but that his reference to depictions of reality make it certain that he is thinking in terms of the same literary principles.[6] Ōiwa also sees the thoroughly believable plot of "The Second-story Window" as providing a model for Hakuchō's Naturalistic fiction, for Hakuchō calmly and evenly depicts simple domestic situations and unromantic love affairs.[7]

"The Second-story Window" is another story told by a first-person narrator, but it is a decidedly different type of story from "Discord and Harmony." It begins on graduation day at the university where the narrator has just completed his third year of study. He says of himself that he has no relatives, little money, and must spend yet another long summer in his lodgings although all of the other students have gone elsewhere for the vacation.[8]

His whole world consists of what he can see from the window of the second-story four-and-one-half mat room he rents. Looking out his window he can see Mt. Fuji, the lightning rod of his university, another second-story window, and the smokestack of a factory. Below he can also spy on the comings and goings of the poor people of his neighborhood. More is told about the problems of these people he observes than about himself.

To dispel his loneliness he spends his mornings reading the romances of Scott. The novelist who lives in the room below chides him for reading such fantastic literature. He tells him that what he sees on the street is reality, but what he reads in Scott's novels is meaningless fantasy. The romance of Scott is contrasted with the seamy reality of life on the street. But when the married couple across the street, whose frequent quarrels had been the object of much of his attention, move away, the student buries himself in more reading of Scott to survive the summer.

Exactly what this is supposed to mean is unclear, but the implication is that such Romantic literature is no more than an escape from life's reality. "The Second-story Window" is another stage in the development of the fictional style and philosophical attitude that would characterize "Dust."

III *"Old Friend" (1906)*

Hakuchō's fourth story, "Old Friend," appeared in *Shinshō-setsu* in September, 1906, coincidentally in the same issue with Natsume Sōseki's *Kusamakura* (Grass Pillow). "Old Friend" is told from the third-person point of view. Whereas "Discord and Harmony" was a first-person story that might better have been third-person, the reverse seems true in "Old Friend." At least, the narrator of "Old Friend" has only limited knowledge of his characters' thoughts; we are given only the thoughts of one character — Seiichi. Events are seen through Seiichi's eyes and we get a hint of their effect upon him more than upon the other characters. The strain of the third-person mode upon an essentially first-person perception is apparent at the conclusion of the story as Seiichi seems to become the third-person narrator.

Seiichi is a young man in his twenties who is concluding six months of travel in Southern Japan with a visit to an "old friend," Inamura, in Nara. Inamura has been married for several years to O-Sen, the daughter of the man Seiichi calls "Uncle." This "uncle" had taken the orphan Seiichi into his home and raised him like a son. He had also insisted that Seiichi adopt the Christian religion as his own children did. Life in his household was characterized by regular prayer gatherings, Bible reading, and constant reaffirmation of each member's Christian faith. Until adulthood Seiichi truly believed in Christianity, but we learn he has abandoned it some three years before the events of the story. "Uncle" had intended him to use his education to spread Christ's word, but instead he had become the English language reporter for a magazine.

Inamura had been a promising painter in Tokyo. He was talented, effusive, confident, and ambitious. His marriage to the beautiful O-Sen had only seemed to add to his good fortune and bright future. However, many months after marrying, he quickly became taciturn and diffident. Finally, he moved to Nara — Siberian exile to the young Meiji provincial Hakuchō. He has turned his back upon worldly ambition. He conducts unhurried research upon the historical artifacts and Buddhist remains of the ancient capital. Meanwhile, O-Sen languishes in her lonely life of exile cut off from the activity of Tokyo. Inamura is determined never to return to Tokyo and his former pretensions; O-Sen is on the point of leaving him.

Behind all of this appears to be Inamura's "secret" — a shameful burden he apparently acquired after marrying O-Sen and that he will never reveal. We are never told exactly what this secret is, but we are told another "secret" that must be directly related to the first. This is Seiichi's secret: he had witnessed a pledge of love between O-Sen, seventeen at the time, and Sakawa, a man described as the most carefree and pleasure-seeking of all the young Christians who learned from O-Sen's father. Seiichi has chanced to meet this Sakawa again just before coming to Nara. In the ten years since he parted from the young O-Sen, Sakawa has lived with at least five women and held any number of menial jobs. When Seiichi saw him, he was tipsy as always.

Toward the close of "Old Friend," O-Sen becomes seriously ill. In pain and in fear for her life, she seeks to embrace the Christianity that she has confessed to Seiichi a few days earlier she never believed, even as a child. She has Seiichi reading the Gospel of John to her; she longs to hear her father pray again. Seiichi recalls his own similar feelings when seriously ill many years before; he assumes it is merely her illness driving her to Christianity and he proves correct. When she recovers, she loses her recent religious fervor and merely wants to return to the excitement of Tokyo. Seiichi says goodbye to his old friends and heads back to Tokyo, dramatically bidding adieu to all the rustic diversions he has seen in his travels.

Oh, Nara, discarded object! Farewell! Oh, mountains and streams of Kyushu and Shikoku that have watched over me for half a year! Farewell! Seiichi felt his heart throb at each station he passed.[9]

Quoting such a passage is perhaps unfair to "Old Friend." However, the posturing of this ending, ornate language as the story opens, and devices such as the "secrets" that cannot be revealed but alter character are probably what lead Ōiwa to see the story as a reversion to earlier more "Romantic" fiction. Of Hakuchō's more important earlier stories, Ōiwa sees "Solitude," "Discord and Harmony," and "Old Friend" to be reminiscent of the style of Ozaki Kōyō (1867–1903), against whose flowery fictional style Japanese Naturalism was in part a reaction. "The Second-story Window" and "Dust" Ōiwa sees as of the same stripe as the realistic works of Doppo.[10] As always, Hakuchō is both romantic and realist.

"Old Friend" is another long story, fifty-two pages as it

appeared in *Shinshōsetsu*. Like "Discord and Harmony" and "The Second-story Window," it was not felt to merit inclusion in Hakuchō's *Complete Works*. Nevertheless, I find these early stories of significance. Hakuchō's youthful Christian faith of the 1890s is always described as strong and fervent. If so, it would seem odd to find it absent from his writing of the next decade. Obviously, it is not absent, by any means. The frequency of Christian elements in Hakuchō's earliest stories is evidence of the great impact they had upon him as a young man. This would seem to make his eventual return to Christianity less puzzling.

In "Old Friend" Hakuchō tries to evoke both the tranquil majesty seen in the Buddhist temples of Nara and the power of Christianity to move one through guilt. The guilt of the Christian is due to his sinfulness. It is guilt toward God the Father for being offensive in His eyes: for having fallen from a state of grace and occasioned the death of His Son Jesus. Seiichi's own spiritual "anguish" comes from guilt toward his "Uncle" — a surrogate father who has provided for him but is demanding and specific in his expectations. "Uncle" is like the Christian God in his eyes; he is indebted to him but is aware that he is not his real father. In a way, this hints at the dilemma of the Japanese Christian: namely, his consciousness of Christianity as an alien religion with which he is somehow uncomfortable despite its many consolations and attractions.

The Christian sense of guilt shown in "Old Friend" is reinforced through association with the Japanese concept of *on*, or obligation. Seiichi tells O-Sen he has incurred great indebtedness (literally, a "great *on*" — "*taion*") to her father.[11] He fears he will be thought "one who doesn't know *on*" ("*on-shirazu*")[12] for having forsaken Christianity, Uncle's religion.

The attitude of the characters of "Old Friend," especially Seiichi, toward religion in general and Christianity in particular reveals Hakuchō's own attitude. This seems a safe statement, for most aspects of this attitude are reiterated in his later writing, including, significantly, his essays. Related to our discussion of Christian guilt is that of the fearful quality of sin. When Seiichi chanced to look out upon the moonlit garden to see and overhear O-Sen and Sakawa, the innocent Seiichi's reaction was as follows:

To Seiichi it was just as if some secret of his own had been found out. He grew pale and staggered to a chair. He wept and prayed to God. Through the open window the moonlight streamed about his feet; the silent wind quietly moved the pages of Dods[13] that lay upon his desk. He recalled the sermon of Pastor Iwai the day before: "God is eternally good; Nature is eternally pure; what is foul is man; the evildoers are the descendants of Adam." He wondered whether the Devil had invaded even the home of his saintly Uncle; for the first time he felt the horror of the sin of the world.[14]

Thus, Hakuchō is concerned with a conception of sin involving man's irremediable loss of innocence deriving from the fall of Adam, in short, original sin.

The characters in "Old Friend" regard Christianity as a severe religion that seems at odds with man's basic social instincts. As we have seen, it was the severity of Meiji Japanese Christianity, as much as anything, that drove Hakuchō away. Hakuchō's first exposure to Christianity was through Protestant missionaries; the faith of the early missionaries to Japan was, in the view of Japanese scholars, characterized by its New England Puritanism.[15]

During the period of Hakuchō's most intense faith — his early years in Tokyo — he was under the influence of Uchimura Kanzō. Uchimura's own faith was largely characterized by similar Calvinist views; Uchimura studied in New England, at Amherst College among other places. The religious view he acquired included a strong sense of righteousness[16] and of the importance of original sin.[17] Thus, a reaction to Uchimura's beliefs, more than to his personality or reputation, was probably involved in Hakuchō's rejection of Christianity.

As young Hakuchō himself had, the fictional Seiichi feels that Japanese Christianity does not prepare one for dealing with Japanese society, When he goes to work at the magazine, he discovers how humorless he is in comparison with his jovial colleagues. He makes what for the young man seems a significant realization: "There is no humor in the Bible."[18]

Christianity is frightening in its concepts and severe in its precepts. In "Old Friend" Hakuchō is probing in what even he considered the logical quarter for a Japanese — Buddhism. He is aware of the calm spell with which it can transfix its believers; this is represented by the ancient Buddhist institutions of Nara. Inamura, the "old friend," is under this spell; it alone seems to enable him to bear the weight of his personal secret. However, for Seiichi Buddhism is a relic whose need is no longer felt. Buddhism is not a real philosophical alternative for the modern Meiji man. This is not a surprising view for the young provincial Hakuchō — who left Christianity to see more of the world, who faulted the Christians for ignoring the "new" knowledge. For Hakuchō at this time, Buddhism seemed, in short, old-fashioned.

Hakuchō was not alone among his peers in feeling the impossibility of religious belief in late Meiji Japan. Perhaps this was the harvest of the ideas sown in the 1880s and 1890s, when Western scientific method and pragmatic thought were officially encouraged and widely accepted. Certainly doubt was the central attitude of the Japanese Naturalists, who were by now in the first stages of their rapid formation and emergence.

Hōgetsu, the theoretician of the Naturalists, had said that although believing in something offers a kind of peace, the age no longer permitted the continuation of belief. The age permitted only doubt and confession. It was felt that all thought beyond that failed to penetrate the essense of reality. Doubt was not the end in itself, for Hōgetsu held that in doubt there still remains in some form or other the desire and endeavor to know the limits of doubt. Hōgetsu saw the paradoxical desire to know the unknowable as the essence of creation. Hakuchō and the other Naturalists agreed with Hōgetsu's skeptical conclusions about the nature of knowing and human existence.[19]

Belief was impossible, but it was enviable, nonetheless. As seen in the illness of O-Sen, for Hakuchō the attraction of Christianity lay in its power to free its believers from the fear of death. I have alluded to the prominence such fear may have held in Hakuchō's thoughts, and to his own experiences with prayer during illness. Christianity was valuable in times of crisis, but of little use normally. Hakuchō seemed to admire the serenity and strength it brought in the face of death, but the young Hakuchō was interested in life. The Christian seemed isolated. Within fifteen years, Hakuchō would be seeking philosophical solitude, but in 1906 such isolation seemed a desolate, rather than splendid, intellectual position. This seems apparent in "Old Friend" when Seiichi and Inamura discuss Seiichi's own flight from the Christianity Uncle taught them.

"Yes, I gave it up three years ago."

"But you were so devoted; your religion was your life. It must have been painful to leave it."

"You're right. It hurt for a while, but I'm over that now. Because it's as you've long said: the church today is just the corpse of religion. It's sad, because Uncle is as zealous as ever, but one by one, all the young men he instructed have betrayed him.''

"But your uncle has never wavered and he's lived up to his religion so faithfully, so he's all the happier.''

"That's right, because he's unaware of them himself, and imagines that he's scoring triumph after triumph. But the young men who used to gather every Saturday at Uncle's house — Hikawa, Tsukahara, you remember all the 'revival' commotion when those mighty fanatics got together. Even that cynic Shiraita was one of the zealots. They all thought they could live on faith alone, but now the fire has gone out. Only Uncle is left — the keeper of the tomb.''

"The keeper of the tomb?" Inamura muttered. "But everything is like that. Glory, enterprise — in the end they're just whitewash on the tomb. People clamor after them, and that's life. It's absurd, absurd,'' he sighed.

"You sound like some monk!'' Seiichi said with a smile.[20]

Inamura is a Buddhist, if only by default. At least he utters essentially, though not perhaps exclusively, Buddhist sentiments about the futility of attachment to this life. However, he cuts an unenviable and forlorn figure like the relics of Nara as seen in "Old Friend.'' He recognizes this miserable aspect of his Buddhist convictions, when he seems to envy the self-assurance of Uncle's Christian self-righteousness.

Buddhism was a relic; Christianity was too removed from reality. Philosophically, Hakuchō was left with only this life. That would be the domain of the Naturalist writer in Japan, as it had been in the West. The Western Naturalist — Émile Zola, for example — had tried to depict objective reality on a vast, impersonal scale, whereas the Japanese, including Hakuchō, was led to a tighter, more personal focus. Despite their many well-known differences, however, they may have shared a bond in their common rejection, in the main, of the supernatural.

IV   *"Dust" (1907)*

"Dust" (February, 1907) is a brief story, which focuses on two characters. The story is set in a dingy newspaper office crowded with reporters; the time is a few days before the New Year. The gray mood of the story contrasts with the more festive air the Japanese reader associates with the approach of the holiday season.

The cinematic, modern nature of the story is evident from the opening paragraph. It begins with an editor shouting that the copy is ready and continues with a description of the stifling atmosphere of the crowded office stuffy from the heat of the stove in winter. As in a 1930s Hollywood movie, atmosphere is produced by the inclusion of superfluous characters. There is the notion that the unhealthy atmosphere destroys everyone. They are all simply "withering in installments,"[21] for most people are denied the beauty of an early death, and are fated to wither, to grow old and die.

The story is told in the form of a first-person narrative by a young proofreader, who is twenty-four. He describes his general insignificance and low social position, as well as how he had once tried to emigrate to South America but still has far-fetched dreams about a bright future for himself. He is contrasted with another character, fellow proofreader Ono, an older man of drab appearance and taciturn manner who has been with the newspaper more than thirty years.

The central incident of the story consists of the young man inviting Ono to have a few drinks with him after work. After another conversation between a couple of reporters in which one, who is described as usually jovial, relates the futility of his work — he works hard, but all he gets are colds and diarrhea — the young man and Ono go out drinking. The bleakness of winter and the cause for reflection on what one has achieved that the year's end brings seem to cast an air of melancholy over everyone's thoughts.

When they are finally settled in an inexpensive restaurant (when asked where he would like to go Ono answers only some place cheap), the young man notes that Ono is like a lifeless statue. His eyes are dull and he has been totally enervated by his decades of monotonous and meaningless work at the newspaper office. The *sake* they drink allows Ono to relax and to become more communicative, however. He is able to relate how he had hopes for his life when a young man but is now little more than an automaton in the employ of his newspaper. Ono has been completely destroyed by the routine of his work, and the young narrator seems perceptive enough to see Ono as an image of what he himself would be like were he to resign himself to a lifetime of proofreading.

Masamune Hakuchō is at times described as an Existentialist writer.[22] The whole philosophy of "Dust," and especially the characterization of Ono, is a good example of what might lead Japanese critics to refer to Hakuchō's writings in Existentialist terms. After presenting his bleak situation and philosophy to the narrator, Ono says of himself, "I keep thinking that the only thing I have to be thankful for is that I'm alive."[23] The following day when the two meet again at work Ono is his old laconic self, wrapped in his attitude of resignation and indifference. The narrator must perform his monotonous tasks again that day as usual; he closes his story with the comment, "I consoled myself thinking I have a future."[24]

The lifeless Ono seems to represent the reality of despair, whereas the young first-person narrator embodies the illusion of hope. We know that the story is to some extent autobiographical; we could give in to the temptation to view the narrator simply as Hakuchō. But viewing the story as a separate fictional reality, we can only assume that the odds are against the young hero really escaping the dust of the grimy workaday world Hakuchō describes. He still has his hopes for the future to console him, but Hakuchō tells us little about him to indicate that he is different from the mass of humanity, that he will succeed in escaping the process of "withering in installments," where others have failed.

"Dust" is, thus, important for two reasons: the triumph of Naturalism and the triumph of skepticism. In "Dust" the realistic method finally wins out; unless we see undue self-pity in the young narrator's conception of himself, "Dust" seems free of earlier Romantic elements. Christianity is also totally and noticeably absent from "Dust." As his Japanese critics all repeat, "Dust" established Hakuchō's reputation as a writer among his literary colleagues. In fact, "Dust" establishes Hakuchō as not just a writer, but as both Naturalist and nihilist.

V *"Ghost Picture" (1907) and "Peace of Mind" (1907)*

"Ghost Picture" (July, 1907) is perhaps the best example among his early stories of Hakuchō caught between realism and fancy. The effect of the story is somewhat like a Zola reworking of a dark story by Poe. To a lesser extent, it recalls the psychological fleshing out of simple tales from Japanese folk literature by Akutagawa Ryūnosuke (1892–1927), although it lacks the conscious artistry of Akutagawa as surely as it does that of Poe.

The hero of "Ghost Picture" is another young painter: Moriichi. He lives in a dingy room in Tokyo. He shuns all companionship; he has no ambition and paints for himself. The only people he has any dealings with are a slovenly old neighbor woman and her daughter

O-Shika. This girl is described in distressing detail: she has one eye, a large protruding tooth, and is a half-wit. She does errands for Moriichi; she is amiable and visits his room freely.

The reasons for Moriichi's reclusive nature are carefully — we might even say "scientifically" — documented. They are hereditary and environmental; they are all traceable to his childhood. It may seem obvious, but must be mentioned, that here Hakuchō resembles Western Naturalist writers, such as Zola. I cannot assert that Hakuchō had in mind the Western writer and his theories of the writer as the scientist among novelists, but Hakuchō had been familiar with Zola for nearly a decade.

Moriichi's father was a drunkard, an enthusiastic one who kept a mistress and was known to dance about his house naked in moments of inebriated ecstasy. Moriichi's mother was, not surprisingly, a nervous wreck, suffering fits of *hisuterii* (hysteria), to quote the Japanese term. Young Moriichi was ignored; he became withdrawn and solitary. Only an interest in painting tied him to life, but even this bond was a weak one. As a youth he was once restrained, by his father, when on the point of shooting himself with his father's pistol.

His father died, his mother committed suicide, and Moriichi used his inheritance to go to Tokyo to study art. The excitement of this move was only a momentary distraction and he soon settled into a dark existence. A visit by Kirishima, a fellow artist, is described. He attempts to draw Moriichi into society — or just out for a walk — but is brusquely rejected. A later visitor is an attractive young woman reporter, who has romantic designs upon him. She has come often before, but Moriichi is always unfriendly. Their conversation when Moriichi unwillingly greets her reveals his character:

"Is there something you need?" he said bluntly.

"Nothing in particular; I happened to be in the neighborhood." She raised her gaze slightly and looked at him boldly.

"I don't feel well. If you want to talk, please come some other day."

"You never feel well, do you? When do you think you might feel better?"

"I'll feel better when I'm dead."

"Dead, dead. You always talk so easily about dying. You're peculiar because you're always thinking about such nonsense. Why not go for a walk along the Edo? I'll go with you. Come on — just once would be alright, wouldn't it? I've asked you so many times; you could at least go out with me once."

"Is it so nice outside? Kirishima wanted me to go with him to the Edo; the lady next door wanted me to come look at cherry blossoms..." Moriichi said as if talking to himself.

"They're at their best right now along the Edo. And the moon is nice; it's so boring to stay in the house on a night like this!"

"In that case perhaps you'd better go by yourself." (*MHZ,* I, 41–42)

"Ghost Picture" is a brief work. There is not time to develop more than one character. The woman is one of many characters Moriichi rejects as he moves rapidly toward psychosis. When the woman finally reaches out and touches him, Moriichi is startled. At that instant the last links with reason seem broken: he imagines that the reporter is the odious mistress of his dead father, so he knocks her down and bolts out into the street. He suffers a further humiliation at the hands of some young men in a coffee shop; he returns to his room when he is certain the young woman has gone.

When he enters his room he quickly destroys and discards a hideous likeness of his father he has painted. He hears the idiot girl singing outside; her singing has meant little to him before but now he is moved to tears by its artless sorrow. She soon finds her way to his room. In characteristically discreet Meiji fashion, we move to a new chapter and find Moriichi waking up the next morning. He is horrified to recall what he did the night before with the idiot girl. He had resolved to be the last of his family; with that line would die the hated memories of his parents. Most horrifying to him now is the thought that the idiot girl could bear his child.

He confronts her with his father's pistol; he will first kill her and then himself. He loses heart; he drops the gun and moves to his veranda. The idiot girl picks up his gun out of curiosity: it accidentally discharges, the bullet striking Moriichi in the head. As his final chapter, Hakuchō adds a brief, ironic postscript.

Kirishima took care of the burial. The unfinished "Pandemonium" was shown, by him, at an exhibition of paintings. It was judged a work of genius by the fickle world.

Shingō Moriichi left no descendants, but, thanks to his painting, a mere whim of his, his name lives on despite him. (*MHZ,* I, 45)

The specter of Moriichi's father haunts "Ghost Picture." It is a portrait of his father that Moriichi destroys as events approach their climax. For Hakuchō, the father figure is a source of fear and chaos rather than of security and order. It is a thoroughly secular story, however. We need not bring the Judeo-Christian God the Father into this discussion.

Moriichi's union with the idiot girl grows out of his impotent rage. He vents the fury of his thwarted instincts upon an object, the girl, rather than upon a person. His experiences with people — parents, painters, women, neighbors, strangers — have been humiliating and painful. He has sought to withdraw totally from life. The morning after, however, he imagines that even the idiot girl, whom he had exempted from humanity, betrays him through her female fertility.

He is unable to fire his father's pistol, a weapon symbolic of the somehow destructive male sexual urges that created him. Not only is he unable to kill the girl, but underlying this is his inability to kill himself. However, we are told, he lost the courage to die after the death of his father, which removed the symbol of his shameful human insignificance.[25]

Thematically, "Ghost Picture" resembles the later "Illusion." As we shall see, in each story the hero rejects the usual paths to peace and is left with only death to confront. Both heroes are convinced that death will end existence. Both willingly proceed to the threshhold of death (and nonexistence), but find themselves at the last moment reluctant to cross over. Both are given a shove at that point: surrealistically in "Illusion" and, less effectively, by the ironic deus ex machina (the accidental shooting) in "Ghost Picture."

The difference between the two treatments of this theme of the reluctant Existentialist lies in the psychological context of "Ghost Picture" and the philosophical context of "Illusion." The change in frame of reference illustrates the transformation in Hakuchō's thought between 1907 and 1922, to which we earlier referred. In "Ghost Picture" Hakuchō is part Naturalist and part writer of fantasy; in "Illusion" he abandons himself completely to fantasy and Surrealism.

Perhaps more significant than style is the fact that in both stories Hakuchō draws the same Existential conclusion: with death man ceases to exist, so that he knows and is concerned with only himself and, ultimately, controls his own existence. Hakuchō does not see this view as offering peace to man in this life — in this case, his only life — because it occasions apprehension and uncertainty about the character of nonexistence. The "inevitable" conclusion is, thus, no resolution; in both stories Hakuchō is reluctant to accept the "inevitable."

"Peace of Mind" (June, 1907) is a first-person account of a devout young Japanese Christian tormented by an awareness of his own sinfulness and unworthiness. He is a valued member of his congregation. He is admired by the other members, as is their pastor, Reverend Shibatani. The source of the young man's anxiety is the uncontrollable lust he feels for some of the women he sees at church — specifically the young organist, Miss Satomi, and the beauty of the congregation, Mrs. Kuroda.

The image of Christianity in "Peace of Mind" is impossible to understand without bearing in mind the influence of Puritanical New England Calvinist attitudes upon Meiji Japanese Protestantism. We have seen this influence upon Uchimura Kanzō. The story's congregation appears to be Presbyterian, and as such may be inspired, to some extent, by that of Uemura Masahisa. Christianity is severe; as in "Old Friend," it sets the believer in opposition to his positive natural instincts — in terms of both personal emotions and social views.

Non-Christian Japanese society as a whole is aware of shame. Had the young man consciously and publicly expressed his desire for Mrs. Kuroda, he would have breached convention. He would have experienced shame at the thought of his lowered status in the eyes of others. The Christian, however, also feels guilt produced by an awareness of his lust, even if (as in "Peace of Mind") it remains secret and occurs in spite of himself. The consciousness is at war with the subconscious, not at one with it. The Christian must subdue the subconscious because man is sinful and impure by nature, as we also saw in "Old Friend."

Public confession before the congregation is the custom in the young man's church. The faithful find him devout because he confesses his sins with great remorse although his "sins" are but faults at worst, not true transgressions of God's law. For example, he once confesses:

"Last Sunday a friend of mine heard the cherry blossoms at Ueno were in full bloom, and he came to invite me to go see them. The weather was good and my head ached a little from a lack of sleep the night before, so I felt like skipping church for one night and going for a walk. I went out with him, but on the way I suddenly realized how weak my faith was and turned back. These things happen to me often."[26]

Common sense tells us he cannot confess his lust for Mrs. Kuroda, whose husband is a revered church elder, to the whole congregation; that is obviously unwise and absurd. Nor is it a Christian act to destroy the equilibrium of the entire congregation to achieve total honesty. However, as Hakuchō seems to perceive the dictates of Christianity, the Christian strives for such spiritual purity. It is the illogicality and impossibility of this, as much as anything, that repels Hakuchō. Hakuchō is preoccupied with the sternness of the Christian God, the special difficulties of public confession for the Japanese, and the darkness of viewing man as sinful. It is idle speculation, but Hakuchō's life might have differed greatly had he been exposed, instead, to the spirit of Roman Catholicism with its gentle Madonna, private confession, and comparatively forgiving attitude toward sinners.

The Reverend Shibatani is another father figure. He stands above the young narrator, but in a fast-moving, even sketchy, conclusion to "Peace of Mind" his character is given an ironic twist. He becomes the light of the young man's salvation — not in the next life, but in this one. He descends to the young man's level and thus brings him peace of mind. Shibatani is seriously ill with influenza. He is near death and the congregation is taking turns watching by his bedside. He has been delirious for some time, and the faithful are awed by the fact that his delirious talk is full of the love of God. Finally, it is time for the tormented narrator and his best friend, Murakami, to take their turn at Shibatani's bedside.

The pastor was sound asleep. We prayed together in silence. We were concerned about his condition, but as the night wore on Murakami began to doze off. I was kept awake by thoughts of how my base heart differed from the pastor's beautiful life. I gazed at the face of the sick man; he writhed a bit in apparent pain: God! Lord Jesus! he called out several times. I straightened the sick man's pillows and replaced the covers that had fallen off. I listened humbly to his delirious speech. He spoke, in a whisper, of the lewdest things imaginable. After a while, he again fell into a deep sleep. I was aghast. I looked back and forth between the pastor's face in sleep and that of Murakami. The name of Mrs. Kuroda had come out repeatedly in that delirious talk! I shook Murakami to awaken him.

"Hey! Didn't you hear that just now?"

"Is something wrong with Sensei?" he answered rubbing his sleepy eyes.

"Too bad you missed it."

I told nothing, not even to Murakami. It goes without saying I will not tell the congregation, either. However, thanks to that vigil, I myself have received a great gift. The delirious talk of Pastor Shibatani was a greater consolation to me than sermons, the lives of the saints, fasting, or prayer. I feel as if my great burden of many months was suddenly lightened. I am not going to Hell alone.[27]

(The End)

CHAPTER 3

Naturalistic Stories

I   *Japanese Naturalism*

DETAILED comparison of Japanese and Western Naturalism is
beyond the scope of this study, but a few words should be said.
In general, Naturalists in both Japan and the West viewed themselves as searching for truth through the faithful re-creation of
objective reality in their art. However, although Western Naturalists, such as Zola or Frank Norris, attempted re-creations of vast
areas of nature and society, Japanese Naturalists characteristically
focused on individual dramas, frequently their own.

Japanese Naturalists, unlike Zola in the 1870s and 1880s, did not
perceive themselves as "scientists," bringing the wisdom of
nineteenth-century science to the literary sphere. On the contrary,
they freely employed a subjective, intimate view of their fictional
material. Although not totally unaware of such concepts, Japanese
Naturalists did not attempt the depictions of the workings of Dar-
winian notions of biological or socioeconomic determinism that
Western Naturalists such as Zola, Norris, or Jack London did.

Commentators in the West have varied only somewhat in their
assessments of the degree of difference between Japanese and
Western Naturalism. For example, one states that "From the first,
Japanese Naturalism was very different from its European counterpart and model."[1] Another concludes a detailed study of Japanese
Naturalism by referring to the "partial misnomer of naturalism."[2]
The "misnomer" is only a "partial" one, for he has found some
similarities to add to the well-known differences. Another notes
that Japanese Naturalism "lacked any intellectual foundation," so
that "Hence there were no Japanese naturalists comparable in
stature to Zola, Flaubert, and Maupassant."[3]

Rather than say that Japanese Naturalism had no intellectual foundation, it might be more accurate to say it had a different intellectual foundation from Western Naturalism. Japanese Naturalism lacked a "scientific" sense, but certainly Naturalists such as Hakuchō and Hōgetsu had a philosophical dimension. They negated all existing philosophical explanations as an intellectual premise, which made their starting point similar to that of Western Naturalists. However, whereas Western Naturalists then embraced science as their new religion, Japanese Naturalists wrote without such a fixed philosophical viewpoint.

It is easy to see how such philosophical independence could soon evolve into a form of Existentialism, as it did in Hakuchō's case. Also, it must have been this philosophical idiosyncracy of Japanese Naturalists that made their non-Naturalistic contemporaries feel threatened by their new writing.

Both Japanese and Western Naturalists were pessimistic, but they derived their nihilism from different sources. Japanese Naturalists considered only their own real-life experiences, which provided them with impulses toward both positive and negative conceptions of reality. For this reason, many Naturalist stories conclude on an open-ended, ambiguous note. That the balance between optimism and pessimism is usually tilted toward the latter shows the inability of individual experience alone to provide a basis for hope.

Different conclusions can be drawn from the pessimism of Western Naturalism, however, for its presence indicates the inability and failure of science to provide a justification for philosophical optimism. The Western Naturalist, under the influence of nineteenth-century Darwinism, viewed man as just another species of animal. In such a view there was no demonstrable proof of the existence of a special source of hope for man.

Hakuchō's frequent use of murder, insanity, and cynicism in his Meiji and Taishō writings illustrates the inability of skepticism and positivism to provide the hope of spiritual peace Hakuchō sought throughout the sixty years of his literary career. Examination of the lives and writing of other Naturalist figures such as Hōgetsu would undoubtedly reveal similar frustration.

In Japan as well as in the West "naturalism represents more a constant wrestling with the spirit of romanticism than a victory over it."[4] The "Romantic" element of Japanese Naturalism is the subjectivity — the self-pity, the posing — inherent in autobiographical writing, often even when it is cast in the form of a third-person narrative. Hakuchō was capable of considerable detachment and distance from his writing, but he frequently disdained it. At times, he even indulged in the posing and self-pity found in the writings of other Naturalists such as Shūsei and Tayama Katai.

Japanese Naturalism is different from its Western counterpart, but it shares many of its problems. The character of Japanese Naturalism, free of comparisons, seems of more immediate importance.

The term "Naturalism" (*shizenshugi*) began to be applied with frequency by the Japanese to their own literature after the appearance of Tōson's *Hakai* (Broken Commandment), as we have seen. Despite *Hakai's* many flaws, it was epoch-making in that, with the exception of Futabatei Shimei's *Ukigumo* (Drifting Cloud) in 1887, it was the first Japanese novel that was modern in spirit. It represented a movement toward the development of characterization and plot and away from the simple emphasis on theme and style characteristic of the *kannen shōsetsu* (idea fiction).[5]

Unlike *Ukigumo*, *Hakai* had a tremendous and immediate impact upon Japanese fiction. It constituted a brief but genuine literary revolution, lasting barely a year or so. However, it was soon inundated by the rush of a newer and greater revolution brought about by the publication of Katai's *Futon* (The Bed) in August, 1907.[6]

Hakai represents the appearance of a modern, large-scale novel which does not appear to be autobiographical.[7] It is fiction in perhaps its truest sense, a creation of the imagination with an imagined plot and imagined characters. The intellectual tension in Japanese fiction after the appearance of *Futon* lay between this familiar approach of *Hakai*, now made in realistic rather than Romantic style, and the new approach of *Futon*.

The frank, obvious autobiographical element in *Futon* made the work a sensation; in it Katai appears to make a total revelation of his inner life by revealing personal attitudes and embarrassing actions that give the work the air of a confession. The literary effects of *Futon* were twofold. First, the distance between the writer and his fictional hero was eliminated. Secondly, fiction became "subjective reflections" that permitted no imaginary hero; the story became the author's, or hero's, monologue.[8]

The problem of aesthetic distance in *Futon* was recognized immediately by contemporary Japanese critics. The October, 1907, issue of *Waseda Bungaku* carried the *"Futon* gappyō" (A Joint Review of *Futon*) which contained articles on *Futon* of varying length by nine critics.[9] Some of these critics such as Oguri Fūyō and Matsuhara Shibun felt that Katai had succeeded in touching reality and discovering a new stylistic technique to free fiction from the hold of the third-person point of view. Others, such as Katakami Noboru, however, noted that Katai was too close to his subject matter. Mizuno Yōshū felt that Katai lacked a critical perspective in *Futon* inasmuch as he was so close to his material.[10]

We must agree with both of these lines of criticism. Our difficulty then becomes one of translating Japanese literary classifications and distinctions into Western literary terminology. The subjective autobiographical "I" novel, begun by *Futon,* might easily be placed in the category of nonfiction by the Western critic. However, essays (*zuihitsu*) and chronicles of impressions (*kansō*) that would possibly be considered nonfiction in the West constitute a large proportion of the body of Japanese fiction (*shōsetsu*).[11]

In the case of *Futon,* then, the reader, Japanese or Western, senses that he is indeed reading something real and true to life and is moved accordingly. At the same time, however, for the Western reader at least, there is the lingering feeling that ultimately his emotions are being manipulated unfairly and that to label such a frankly autobiographical work as *Futon,* or many of Hakuchō's works, as fiction somehow violates the spirit of that term.

Part of the problem lies in the custom of translating the Japanese term *shōsetsu* as "novel" or even as "fiction." The Japanese word seems to include much more territory than the former English term and territory much different from the latter.

Masamune Hakuchō was one of the nine contributors to the *"Futon* gappyō." His criticism was brief but characteristically incisive. To Hakuchō *Futon* was a masterpiece in which Katai finally succeeded in producing an important work of fiction which truly realized the possibilities of his announced artistic intentions and fully incorporated his fictional theories.[12] Hakuchō noted that *Futon* was an original work, showing no signs of borrowing from a foreign literary source.

In discussing the historical significance of *Futon,* Hakuchō ranked the evolution of Katai's fictional style alongside Tsubouchi Shōyō's redefinition of the purposes of fiction in his *Shōsetsu shinzui* (The Essence of the Novel) of 1885 and Kosugi Tengai's call for an objective fictional realism in the preface to his *Hatsu sugata*

(First Appearances) in 1900. Hakuchō also delighted in the fact that Katai did not try to elicit the sympathy of the reader for his hero, and in the fact that Katai did not permit his narrative to stray into the ornate language of his earlier works.[13]

II *"Whither?" (1908)*

The January, 1908, issue of *Waseda Bungaku* was devoted to the problem of Naturalism, or *shizenshugi.* There were five lengthy essays: Hōgetsu wrote on Naturalism in art, Sōma Gyofū on the Naturalism of Maupassant, Nakamura Seiko on the Naturalism of Zola, Katakami Noburu on the Naturalism of Flaubert, and Shiramatsu Nanzan on Naturalism in philosophy. There were, also, two extraordinary examples of Japanese Naturalistic fiction: Katai's "Ippeisotsu" (One Soldier) and the first of four monthly installments of Hakuchō's "Whither?"

Waseda Bungaku was to select "Whither?" and Tōson's *Haru* (Spring) as the best stories of 1908,[14] a year which saw Shūsei's *Arajotai* (New Household), Katai's *Tsuma* (Wife), and Sōseki's *Sanshirō* appear as well. The hero of "Whither?", the world-weary, blasé Suganuma Kenji, appealed to the Japanese intellectual of the day. As Gotō puts it, the period following the Russo-Japanese War was an age of disillusionment, which saw the appearance of a "lost generation" in Japan.[15] Hakuchō's creative sensibility was in tune with the mood of the times.

Gotō does not see "Whither?" as the best of the fictional output in 1908 nor does he feel that its selection was due to the favoritism of the Waseda faction. He sees it as an indication of the difference between then and now in critical standards and audience appeal.[16]

Ōiwa, on the other hand, likes to stress the autobiographical possibilities of the story. He cannot agree with Ara Masahito who holds Kenji to be a composite of the two heroes of two nineteenth-century Russian stories, Pechorin of *A Hero of Our Time* (1840) by Mikhail Yurevich Lermontov and Rudin of *Rudin* (1855) by Ivan Turgenev. He does not see Hakuchō imitating any of the foreign writers with whom he was then infatuated. He characterizes Hakuchō as a man who never fought against his own nature and never tried to change those aspects of his character that needed changing, so that he resembles the hero of "Whither?"[17]

Hakuchō disclaimed that he himself was the model for Kenji, saying simply that he was influenced by "some Russian story."[18]

This vague, offhand admission by Hakuchō plus the fact that Lermontov's *A Hero of Our Time* is credited as being the work that first opened Hakuchō's eyes to the dark philosophical and introspective possibilities of literature[19] make it impossible to ignore the similarities between the dark and egoistic philosophies of Lermontov's Pechorin and Hakuchō's Kenji.

Such a resemblance and the fact that Hakuchō knew *A Hero of Our Time* well do not compel a judgment of slavish imitation, however. Pechorin should be seen as a part of Hakuchō's education and not as a model for Kenji. Hakuchō had little need of foreign models; models were all about him in the disillusioned postwar world of late Meiji Japan.

That Naturalism represents "more a wrestling with the spirit of romanticism than a victory over it" is evident from "Whither?" Kenji is a misunderstood young man, but he does not want to be understood. He is indifferent, self-centered, and self-pitying. He is the clown of his class in college, who neglected his studies but somehow managed to graduate. He worked as a high school teacher, but since quitting has been a reporter. He lives with his father and mother and two younger sisters, Chiyo and Mitsu.

Kenji's friends include: Oda, a responsible young man who struggles with translation work to earn money for his family; Katsurada, a drily serious scholar of about forty; and Katsurada's wife. Oda has an attractive young sister of marriageable age, O-Tsuru. Her future figures prominently in the story.

Oda repeatedly urges Kenji to marry O-Tsuru, but Kenji is not interested in marriage. To Kenji, "human beings are parasites; a woman is a lump of flesh" (*MHZ*, I, 88). He would rather promote a match between her and a more respectable suitor, Minoura. Kenji often buys the company of prostitutes, but his only real communication is with Mrs. Katsurada. She is an intelligent and sensitive woman, withering away as the wife of the unapproachable scholar.

Kenji derives no satisfaction from drinking and from prostitution. He often has fantasies of pleasures beyond his reach, such as opium. At times he imagines himself being blown to bits as a soldier in a revolutionary army or being hanged as a mountain bandit. To Kenji, wars, revolutions, and arctic expeditions are man's way of relieving his boredom.

The extreme world-weariness of the hero, his lack of stimulation — a situation in which even a rash act would not rouse him from his ennui — is this not a somewhat Romantic attitude being taken by the "Naturalistic" author? Kenji's intellectualizing and his awareness of himself remind us of the young hero of "Dust," but their situations are significantly different. Kenji lacks the other man's freshness, the impression of unaffected interest in his own fate that makes it appropriate for the hero of "Dust" even to ask whether there is any hope for him. The "I" of "Dust" is a man with few or no opportunities, whereas Kenji throws away his opportunities in favor of self-pity. Kenji is not victimized by his environment; he is in a hell of his own choosing. In "Dust," however, the young hero, and certainly Ono, have no hope of controlling the effects of their environment upon their lives.

Kenji's father wants him to hasten his marriage, so that the demands of filial piety hang over Kenji's head as further reason to go against his instincts and marry. Kenji has no real communication with anyone. His father, who is ill, waits up for him each night hoping for just a chance to talk to his son, and trying at the same time not to alienate him. Kenji is aware of his concern, but it only serves to irritate Kenji. Kenji finds himself wandering around Oda's neighborhood in an attempt to avoid his father. Kenji feels it is a pity Oda works so much just for his fat wife and family. He views Professor Katsurada and his wife as living in a grave with his wife writhing.

As "Whither?" ends, it looks as if Oda has decided to give O-Tsuru in marriage to someone other than Kenji, namely Minoura. Although he had tried to avoid marrying her, this too upsets Kenji. He wanders off, but to where?

Although the success of "Whither?" in 1908 seems attributable to its appeal to the intellectual mood in Tokyo at the time, it is of autobiographical interest as well. There are links with other Hakuchō stories and with his struggle toward a personal philosophy.

In one scene, for example, Kenji is intrigued by some sidewalk Salvation Army preachers because they believe they have found a philosophical answer. We know that the Naturalists felt that the times did not permit belief, so that the blind faith of these Christians must have seemed incredible to Hakuchō and his more sympathetic readers. This is the blind faith that Hakuchō admired in the medieval man of Japan and Europe.

Of the most impact in 1908 must have been the agonized pose, the psychological sadomasochism of Kenji. In the following scene Hakuchō has just told us that Kenji realizes that, on the whole, he is loved by all of his friends and relatives:

" 'Blessed are the beloved and those who love.' That's the kind of facile maxim saints and poets are fond of uttering. But it's not in the least applicable to me. The more I am loved, the lonelier I feel. My strength ebbs and the feeling of isolation is unbearable. I prefer to be hated and attacked from all quarters — that would arouse some reaction in me. But to be caressed and fondled: a lifeless life, what good would it be? 'Blessed are the persecuted': that suits me better. Let me be tormented and made to cry; let me be wounded and felled: a life filled with life ... that's what I want!" (*MHZ*, I, 73)

Although Hakuchō may have had Dante in mind when speaking of "poets," the saint and poet alluded to is most likely Matthew. The style of the first sentence quoted recalls that of the Bible. At first glance the psychology of Kenji seems a Japanese version of European fin-de-siècle weltschmerz. However, it is also a specific rejection of the spirit of Matthew 5, the Sermon on the Mount.

Both the biblical Christ and Hakuchō's Kenji desire persecution, but Kenji is not a true Christ-figure. To Kenji a life of goodness numbs the senses; he desires decadence and self-abuse to bring his senses to life. He denies his spirituality, which seems nearly dead anyway, in order to experience his physicality. Christ, on the other hand, gave up His physical life for the sake of His spirit. Unlike those of Christ, Kenji's actions are aimed at his own "salvation," not that of others.

Kenji's makeup is different from that of Bunzō in Futabatei's *Ukigumo*. Bunzō's stubborn pride and complex psychology immobilize him and prevent him from showing his affection for his aunt O-Masa and the young girl O-Sei. Kenji, on the other hand, is more of a poseur. Kenji is almost Byronic; he is a self-pitying young man who seeks justification through social persecution.

If Kenji appears to be a Romantic pessimist, it is unintentional. Hakuchō takes pains to disassociate Kenji from romance. In one scene, for example, Kenji has been reading the autobiography of a Russian revolutionary.

He placed the book face down and lay back. He despaired of appreciating the career of a man of different circumstances of distant relation to himself. Then he took the book down from the desk and simply read passages here and there at whim. The parts which spoke of joining ranks with the peasants in revolution and of fleeing the country and wandering in foreign lands were written interestingly. But soon they seemed to lose their luster. They failed to excite Kenji even as much as the tales of desperate Restoration Loyalists he heard from his father as a child. He closed his eyes and let his thoughts wander. There was no shower of sparks on all sides; he heard no battle cries. All that floated through his mind was the sight of people trudging through the rising Ginza dust. (*MHZ*, I, 76)

Hakuchō again uses the symbol of the Ginza dust (*hokori*). This "dust" to Hakuchō seems to be a symbol of a Naturalistic, concrete, objective reality. It is contrasted with the Romantic, imagined, subjective reality of books, art, religion — all that Hakuchō frequently designated man's "dreams" (*yume*). Kenji may be an unconscious Romantic in his agonized pose, but Hakuchō meant to present him as one who faces life's grim reality directly.

Kenji, like the Naturalists, feels the mood of alienation in his society and sees its banality, but he has no solution but psychological detachment and dispassionate observation. However, Kenji's reaction to the prospect that Minoura would receive the hand of Oda Tsuru — the news staggers him — and the open-ended conclusion of the story indicate that Kenji's (and certainly Hakuchō's) estrangement from belief and hope was not total and irreconcilable.

III "Hell" (1909)

The story "Hell" (January, 1909) concerns a young schoolboy who grows progressively paranoid and eventually breaks down in the classroom before his classmates. Insanity had appeared earlier in Hakuchō's works, such as "Ghost Picture," as we have seen; it would be used again in "The Joys of Life" (1924) and "I Killed a Man, And Yet" (1925). "Hell" must have seemed an exciting and modern story when it first appeared.

"Hell" opens with the cold late autumn wind at B Gakuin, a Christian missionary school on the outskirts of a little town in the Chūgoku area of Japan (which includes Hakuchō's native Okayama Prefecture). The time — some "fourteen or fifteen years ago" (*MHZ*, I, 200) — corresponds with the facts of Hakuchō's life, also.

The hero is a sickly adolescent boy, Akiura Otokichi. He does not follow the advice of his doctor, but he blames him for his failure to recover. He finally stops going to the hospital for he fears the medicine will poison him. He fears being crazy like his grandfather or fainting and dying like his grandmother. His earlier childhood fear of strange creatures and demons has been replaced by upsetting thoughts about the laws of heredity, physiological laws, which might threaten him. Solitary reading is his only refuge from his fears.

The other characters include the missionary P and his wife and daughters. They do not take an active part in the action of the story, but simply function as "happy people" to be mentioned in contrast with the troubled Akiura. During the course of the story Akiura becomes the friend of another student, Sano. Sano is remarkable for drawing unflattering caricatures of Akiura in class, abusing Westerners, and making fun of their religion, Christianity.

Another young fellow is Yonematsu, who is the son of a landlord and a youth with a checkered past. He says that he only wants money, that any job that makes him rich will be fine. He talks of geisha, chides Akiura for studying too much, and rattles on about how he will get away some day, to sail away and be a pirate.

A more important character is the woman referred to as the female caretaker. She is still young; she lives alone separated from her husband. Akiura begins to visit her and to rely upon her. She becomes his reluctant confidante.

The woman is a devout Christian and very loyal to the missionary and his family. Akiura tries to convince her she has been duped by them, that she should give up her nun-like existence and go out into the world. Akiura feels that if there were no people, there would be no pain and hardship, and also no hell. She is often startled by his strange ideas, but she hesitates to oppose him because she is aware of his peculiarity and fears upsetting him.

Akiura becomes increasingly isolated until he reaches the point where he is even suspicious of Sano's innocent invitation to take a walk at school. He resists Sano's talk of how Yonematsu, who we know has been visiting the female caretaker, has been having sexual relations with her. This seems to precipitate Akiura's final collapse. In the end he sees something threatening on the mountain by the school and cries, "It's come! Run for it!" (*MHZ*, I, 219). He feels "they" will get him no matter where he goes.

Christian notions are interjected freely into the story of Akiura. Akiura is impressed by the biblical story of Sodom and Gomorrah, and his fear of people seems tied in with his fear of the wrath of God. This idea is a familiar one, but there is not much detail on the interaction between the frightening character of the biblical God and Akiura's psychology.

One general criticism of "Hell" is that it is perhaps impossible to depict the insanity of a supposedly intelligent and complex character such as Akiura in a story less than half the length of "Whither?" Zola required a full-length novel to delineate the decline of Coupeau and Gervaise in *L'Assommoir,* as did Frank Norris for the deterioration of McTeague and Trina in *McTeague.*

Hakuchō gives a wealth of facts but an even greater accumulation of facts is necessary to treat such a subject by factual documentation alone. Zola and Norris are more successful because they follow the lives of their characters over a period of years. Even without great psychological insight the changes in their characters are clear and believable through the weight of facts alone. Hurstwood and Carrie in Dreiser's *Sister Carrie* is another case in point.

The medium of the short story seems inadequate for what Hakuchō attempts in "Hell." However, despite such shallowness, the limited focus of "Hell" does make it an effective portrait of Akiura. Though it may not tell us how he got that way, it is an impressive portrayal of his psychology; it answers the question what, but not the question why.

IV   *"Wasted Effort" (1910)*

The hero of "Wasted Effort" (July, 1910), Sōkichi, like that of "Hell," is insane. Sōkichi is described as a dreamer to whom ten years are like a day as they pass before his eyes. He had heard voices of gods and demons ten years before, saying,

> "Go to America! If you go to America, you can obtain a great fortune. With that money construct a relief station for the poor! Correcting the mistaken policies of the Japanese government and saving the impoverished people of Japan is your mission, Sawai Sōkichi!" (*MHZ,* I, 340–341)

Sōkichi spent his youth in Chūgoku, including a few months in a mental institution. Since then he has been studying Catholicism, while still cherishing his idea of a "relief station for the poor." He envisions this as a many-faceted operation, so that after purifying his heart through religion (Catholicism), he now proposes to study political science. He is undaunted by the ridicule with which others greet his idea of Japan and Russia controlling the world through one great empire.

Sōkichi's thoughts are filled with such political notions as well as a jumble of phenomena from popular Catholicism. His change purse is filled with holy medals, and he treasures his statue of St. Peter, a picture of Mary, and his rosary. These are all of course no indication of psychosis, but he is also frequently bothered by the feeling that he is being followed. He believes there are political agents following him to thwart his plans. He fears being seen through the window; he sometimes hears voices. On one occasion he is in a sort of daze or trance, and he sees foreign multitudes and hears voices praising him and praying.

Sōkichi has acquired a job. He describes himself as a reporter but his duties mainly involve delivering papers and collecting from subscribers. As he becomes absorbed in his imaginary persecutor, he forgets about going to work. He refers to this person as strange and dangerous, perhaps a man or maybe a woman who has been following him around. He had thought he had one friend who understood him, Higasa, but this fellow too soon begins to tire of Sōkichi and his absurd ideas.

Toward the end Sōkichi has his mother stay with him, to his mind so that he may protect her. At times he sits in a daze making the sign of the cross and waving his hand as if warding off something. He is obsessed with the thought that his mother, brother, and sister have something like snakes entwined about their wrists. When he goes from his rented room to his parents' place to live, he stays up all night walking about lighting matches and guarding the place.

Monomania eventually loses out to paranoia. He says he will let Higasa take care of his great political and social operation for a time, while he himself deals with his tormentor.

Finally, Sōkichi is prowling about the house with a lamp one night, checking every nook and cranny, when his mother wakes up and screams at the sight of her son. His father takes the lamp; Sōkichi assures them they need not worry as he will keep "them" out. He takes his statue of St. Peter and makes the sign of the cross respectfully. Sōkichi makes his rounds every night. His father is exasperated at the decline and the loss of this son he had raised, but he does not have him committed.

The Christian elements of "Wasted Effort" are presented as if Hakuchō were trying to disparage the religion by associating it with the absurd Sōkichi. Sōkichi certainly has none of the intensity of the boy Akiura in "Hell." But on closer examination perhaps some of Sōkichi's apparently insane notions are not so absurd in the context of the Japan of 1910.

The political atmosphere of the times was repressive, at least for those whose ideologies, philosophical as well as political, were suspect. It is impossible to say with absolute certainty that Hakuchō was consciously using the paranoia of his story as a metaphor for the political paranoia of the day. Nevertheless, such a supposition is tempting in the light of the government repression of the rights of free speech and of freedom of thought in 1910.[20] It seems naive to suppose that Hakuchō was unaware of and unaffected by the repressive political climate.

Grand altruistic notions are seen as the notions of a madman in the disturbed literary context of "Wasted Effort" and in that of postwar skepticism. No one today is a stranger to the tension between the practical priorities of the modern world and the often obscured moral demands of its nominal religions. No doubt such contradictions as those between the moral dictates of Buddhism and Christianity and the political and social policies of Japan and the West encouraged such writers as Hakuchō in their doubt and nihilism.

Of the most interest in "Wasted Effort" is the further change in Hakuchō's attitude toward Christianity. In "Whither?" Kenji is greatly impressed by the earnest nature of the evangelizing of some street-corner Salvation Army people. Indeed, that is about the only external stimuli to which he ever seems to respond. He is impressed because he sees that, unlike himself, they are really absorbed in what they are doing and convinced that they have the answer (*MHZ*, I, 71–72).

In "Hell" Akiura is linked with the Christian idea of an avenging God. There is mention of the biblical story of Sodom and Gomorrah; Akiura believes the one responsible for his unhappiness is the "omniscient, almighty, merciless God" (*MHZ*, I, 207), since it was He Who created him. Part of the insanity of the dreamer Sōkichi centers on his grandiose altruistic dreams. All of his illogical schemes are prompted by a desire to save the world. He thinks of others and not himself. Such selfless altruism, the doing of good for others, is at the core of Christian ethical philosophy. At least, that is one interpretation of the example of the life of Christ.

In the last years of Meiji Hakuchō can only express such sentiments in the context of insanity. None of the above three fictional heroes fits into society; all three are drawn to Christianity. The progression in their relationship to Christianity is from the admiration of the sincerity of the believer by the socially superfluous Kenji to the rage and despair of the weak and threatened Akiura to the eager acceptance of the harmless madman Sōkichi. Only the insane characters believe. Hakuchō is echoing metaphorically in his fiction what the Naturalists had been stating categorically in their essays: that the age did not permit belief.

The view of Christian faith in particular and of the notion of belief in general grows progressively dimmer from "Whither?" to "Hell" and finally "Wasted Effort." The believers — the Salvation Army people — in "Whither?" may appear absurd and their message go unheeded, but they are a part of life, nonetheless. It is the hero, Kenji, who is alienated.

In "Hell," although the female caretaker proves to be a sinner and Akiura is driven mad in part by his biblical obsessions, Christianity is still not totally discredited. There remains the example of the peace and contentment of the foreign missionary and his family. But, as foreigners, they show that the Christian faith is becoming more remote from and less relevant to Japanese life in Hakuchō's mind.

The climax is reached in "Wasted Effort," where the Christian Sōkichi is the only character who is totally removed from reality, a madman who prowls about the house at night looking into dark corners. Hakuchō is showing in his fiction that belief, which for him meant primarily belief in Christianity, had lost its relevance for him and for late-Meiji Japan.[21]

V *"Faint Light" (1910)*

The heroine of "Faint Light" (October, 1910) is a concubine, O-Kuni. As such, she is a traditional stock character in fiction about prostitutes and kept women. Such stories were common in Meiji, and were often written by so-called Naturalist writers, such as Chikamatsu Shūkō and Tokuda Shūsei. It seems unlikely that Hakuchō attached much importance to this type of story, either his own or those by others.

Hakuchō wrote "Faint Light" in about a week; it was a true pot-boiler.[22] He had lost his job of many years at the *Yomiuri Shimbun* in June, 1910. A change of editors provided a good opportunity for the newspaper to disassociate itself from Naturalism by firing him.[23] Hakuchō had helped to make the *Yomiuri* a major vehicle for the writing of the anti-establishment Naturalists. In particular, Hakuchō felt the new editor liked neither Tōson's *Ie* (Family), which was being serialized, nor the inclusion of stories by Naturalists such as Shūkō and Iwano Hōmei in the weekly arts page Hakuchō headed.[24]

Naturalist "geisha stories" were often autobiographical. "Faint Light" was no exception. In effect, Hakuchō "stole" the model for O-Kuni from Shūkō. After hearing of her from Shūkō, Hakuchō looked her up on his own; in time he was to keep her for a while. The O-Kuni of "Faint Light" is the prostitute O-Miya in Shūkō's "Wakareta tsuma ni okuru tegami" (A letter to My Former Wife), which appeared in *Waseda Bungaku* in April, 1910. Her patron in the Shūkō story, Osada, who is portrayed as an evil character, is Hakuchō.[25] Such was the world of the Naturalist "geisha story."

There is an obvious tie between these stories and the spirit of Edo stories of the "floating world," or "pleasure quarters." Certainly, they seem removed from the spirit of Naturalism. Western Naturalists such as Zola, the Goncourts, and Stephen Crane wrote of prostitutes, and the Goncourts used specific real-life models for these heroines. Still, the Japanese novelist chronicling his own affairs with a prostitute seems of a different breed than the Western Naturalist, who often viewed himself as an objective, scientific, dispassionate observer. Nevertheless, these stories were important to many of the Japanese Naturalists; "Faint Light" deserves at least a brief look.

Young O-Kuni has undergone many trials. When sixteen, she ran away with a lover who soon deserted her. Unwed, she was forced to give away her baby, which still grieves her. Her mother is ill; her older sister once forced her to become the mistress of a hateful fellow by refusing to lend her the small sum of thirty yen.

O-Kuni is being kept by a man named Asakawa, who seems to be growing tired of her. The proprietress of a brothel, the Yoshiya, lurks about tempting O-Kuni with talk of introductions to new and more profitable patrons. O-Kuni trusts only a young boy, who is her frequent companion.

O-Kuni loves her mother and an older sister who has been kind to her. When O-Kuni makes a visit to her home town, however, she is embarrassed to be questioned by her sisters about her activities. While kneeling before the family Buddhist altar, O-Kuni has fantasies of herself as a beautiful young nun.

Under the strain of her shame, she once feels threatened by a

man in the street staring at her, but when her adolescent friend goes
to investigate he finds no one. On another occasion Asakawa
arrives to find her sitting alone in the dark. She is afraid of crowds,
but also afraid of being alone. Although traditional in Japan, concubinage (*mekake*) is never totally condoned. O-Kuni must withdraw and turn inward in the face of social censure.

Not surprisingly, O-Kuni is fatalistic and morbid; she often
thinks of death. She conceives of an ideal death in the traditional
terms of a double love-suicide. She wants to die together with a
man who truly loves her, but there is no such man. She is merely a
plaything to Asakawa and the others; they do not take her
seriously.

As the story ends, O-Kuni has decided to visit the Yoshiya to hear
the details of these other possible patrons. Asakawa has arrived
unexpectedly at that point.

"I don't want to go anywhere anymore. I don't want to see any other
man but you. You don't want to leave me, either, do you? Then shouldn't
we do away with ourselves once and for all?" She spoke calmly.

"You're in an awfully big hurry to die. When the time comes that we
must die, then we'll die. If you just have that resolve, you can put up with
a little hardship."

"No, you're wrong. You think that because you're still inexperienced.
You might think you can, but if you don't die right away when you want to
die, you won't be able to die easily later."

"But just put up with things a little longer; I'm not going to let you
starve to death."

"I know," she said halfheartedly. O-Kuni lowered her eyes; she was
struck by the gloom of the days to come living in that house. "I suppose
you'll only come about once a week."

"Yes, for the time being I can only come about that often."

"Well, what will I do the rest of the time?" she said. She had, as if for
the first time, a vivid picture of her daily life.

"Just go on as you have been for a little longer." (*MHZ,* I, 402)

They continue in that vein. When she protests she has so little
decent clothing, he chides her for wanting death one minute and
new clothes the next. A messenger comes to tell her to come to the
Yoshiya at once. She applies her makeup hurriedly and stops Asakawa who has started to leave.

"I'll be back in a couple of hours, so wait here until I get back. I want to see how things are over there; I'd hate for us to part like this," she said over and over as she descended the stairs looking back at him several times.

In the rickshaw her fancies were like a shower of sparks. What would be waiting for her at the Yoshiya? (*MHZ,* I, 403)

The "faint light" of the title refers to O-Kuni's faint hopes. Such hopes persist even in the face of her past misfortunes and failures and the whole morass of inevitability her present situation and environment represent. Hope is offered by her youth and persistent though usually ineffectual desire to end somehow her life of concubinage.

O-Kuni differs from a Nana in that she is not a femme fatale full of every type of lust and malice. O-Kuni is adrift and can find nothing but straws of hope to clutch. Zola's Nana, on the other hand, is a woman who becomes aware of her power over her environment and, in particular, over the morally weak men she dominates. Nana ultimately destroys herself through her own excess, which weakness she inherited from her drunken father and her slatternly mother. In "Faint Light," however, the deterministic emphasis is on the effects of environment in shaping character rather than on those of heredity. Likewise, there is no clear resolution of O-Kuni's predicament.

Nana is a statement on the decay of the French aristocracy in the 1860s, whereas there is little explicit mention of the social context of O-Kuni's story. To make a case for it as a conscious attack on the low position and exploitation of women in Meiji Japan would be farfetched. Still the story has incidental value as social history because of its depiction of the favored position of men in their sexual relations with women and the utter dependence and helplessness of the latter.

The most likely conclusion that can be drawn from the intentionally ambiguous ending is that O-Kuni will either go back to being Asakawa's concubine, become a prostitute for the Yoshiya proprietress, or be introduced to yet another patron through the Yoshiya. In short, she will never escape her demoralizing, demeaning way of life.

VI   *"Clay Doll" (1911)*

"Clay Doll" (July, 1911) is a fictionalization of Hakuchō's marriage to the young Tsune, as we have seen. The title refers to the immaturity and naiveté Hakuchō found in his bride. Whether read as fiction or as biography, it is an effective portrayal of the psychological problems involved in the traditional Japanese arranged marriage.

The groom Jūkichi (Hakuchō) is past thirty, but the bride Tokiko (Tsune) is but twenty. This plus the fact that Jūkichi has been living for many years in Tokyo, whereas Tokiko is fresh from the provinces, makes communication between the two impossible. Jūkichi is experienced sexually and socially, but emotionally and intellectually Tokiko is but a child. There is a great contrast between his corrupt sophistication and her virginal purity.

Jūkichi agrees to a *miai* (an introductory meeting of prospective marriage partners) with Tokiko, although he is totally indifferent about the whole affair. He has been unemployed for nearly a year and living a lazy life; he sees the practical advantages of marriage and even sees it as the only way of gaining some peace of mind.

When he finally agrees to marry Tokiko, the whole business is somehow unreal to him. He feels as if it were someone else getting married and not himself. He seems to consent as a kind of atonement for all the trouble over his marriage he has caused his friends.

He soon regrets his assent to the marriage, however, and frets over the better girls whom he has let slip away. He finds it strange to think that a haphazard marriage is the end of his dream of finding the right woman for a mutual love relationship.

After their marriage, Tokiko finds out that all the commendable things she has been told about Jūkichi were lies. He will not even take her out for a walk; he tells her to go to see the cherry blossoms by herself, if she wants to see them. He leaves her at home alone and goes stalking about the entertainment districts. He ridicules his wife's immaturity, saying that if he were younger, he could make her his doll and they could play house. She has no experience with men; she does not talk much and does not know Tokyo, so that to Jūkichi she is just a doll.

When she asks the unhappy Jūkichi if anything is troubling him, he answers that his thoughts are not her concern, that it is enough if they just live together. Tokiko is repeatedly told to endure whatever her husband does, so that she tells no one of her difficulties, believing it is a woman's duty to resign herself to whatever married life brings. During a visit to Tokiko's home town her elder sister accuses Jūkichi of not treating Tokiko properly, but their mother simply warns Tokiko of the sad consequences of leaving her husband and not accompanying him back to Tokyo.

When Jūkichi points out to Tokiko that when she is entered in the official family record (thus formalizing their marriage) she will lose her freedom, she replies, "Freedom? What Freedom?" (*MHZ,* I, 446). Her remark is meant to be neither facetious nor sarcastic, but is given innocently and in earnest. Nevertheless, she feels fearful and lonely when she begins to appreciate the permanence of her marriage. Both of them take walks alone; she gets the "dust" (*hokori*) from the streets in her face. She visits a Buddhist temple to pray for her husband and that he will grow to love her.

When she tries to impress upon him the meaning of the fact that she is his wife, he stares at her and thinks how strange it is that she could really be his wife. He feels as if he is only baby-sitting someone's daughter; now with his marriage he is able to savor dissipation for the first time. The story ends on the note that with his frequent absences, Tokiko makes repeated visits to a temple. Unbeknown to Jūkichi, her visits become the talk of the neighborhood.

Hakuchō's objective depiction of the facts of his initially unhappy marriage accounts for the story's interest and credibility, although this same autobiographical aspect was the reason for much of the critical resistance to it when it appeared. But today more than sixty-five years later, the character who seems the more cruelly portrayed is Jūkichi, Hakuchō himself, rather than Tokiko, Hakuchō's wife Tsune.

So many other alienated heroes have appeared since Jūkichi's day that we can easily accept him and perhaps even identify with him. But Jūkichi is not a character who elicits our sympathy. On the other hand, who can fail to sympathize with Tokiko? Her only crime is her simplicity. She is caught between her sincere desire to do what she is told is her duty as a wife and her realization that to do so is almost impossible.

Tokiko's problems are not internal; they are all external. There is nothing to indicate that she produces her own anxieties; left alone she would no doubt function simply but admirably. The problem is the world she lives in, one that makes impossible demands upon her, with which in her essential goodness she feels she must try to comply.

Jūkichi, however, is more complex and seems to create his own problems from within himself and project them onto others. In a way, of course, like Tokiko, he is at odds with his environment, but the physical and psychological demands upon him as a male and the husband are not nearly as great as those upon Tokiko. He always has the bars and prostitutes to escape to, while as a woman Tokiko has only prayer.

Characteristic of these Naturalistic stories, the conclusion of "Clay Doll" is open-ended. We do not know what becomes of Tokiko and Jūkichi. We can look at the story biographically and find that time and Tokiko's perseverance finally wear away Jūkichi's defenses. Just the story, however, leaves us with a sense of Tokiko's lack of freedom, her imprisonment in her role as a dutiful wife, and her hopeless unhappiness. We are left with a sense of the power of environment to shape the course of a man's or a woman's life.

VII   *"Suffocation" (1911)*

The title of "Suffocation" (September, 1911) is misleading; it is not the account of psychological or philosophical crisis we might expect. "Suffocation" is of interest primarily for its Naturalistic style. It lacks the philosophical interest of many of Hakuchō's other stories. It is for this reason, perhaps, that it is mostly ignored by Hakuchō's Japanese commentators.

The story is told in the first person by a young man. He is a brash, self-confident university graduate. He says of himself, "Since coming to Tokyo I have not wanted for the tender talk of women." After then noting how his schoolmates were often disgraced through the discovery of their affairs, although his romances have caused him no complications, he concludes:

> I am happier than my many such friends and there is nothing to stop me from entering a new life from now on.
> I couldn't be satisfied if I didn't always feel I was happier than others. (*MHZ*, I, 461)

His past adventures haunt him, however. He is being encouraged by the wealthy, respectable family of a "good girl," O-Tane, as the story opens. Soon a former lover he had thought he was done with, O-Tama, talks him into seeing her again. O-Tama is from a poor family and has even become a kept woman, but the narrator is helpless to resist her and they begin their affair again.

He is also attracted to O-Tane, but he often finds the atmosphere of her respectable household stifling. Although he finds O-Tama irresistible, he curses her hold upon him, for it will ruin his reputation and his chances for the lucrative match with O-Tane. At the story's end, he seems headed for a permanent break with the wealthier girl. He sells a few books for money to give O-Tama and hurries off to meet her.

"Suffocation" is the best, along with "Whither?", of Hakuchō's early stories of the troubles of a young man of marriageable age. The hero of "Suffocation" is not nearly as introspective or as defiant as Kenji of "Whither?", however. As a result, he is not nearly as memorable a character, either. Nevertheless, the other characters in "Suffocation" assume more life than those of "Whither?"

One such character is a friend, Egawa, who is cynical and, although he tries to mask it, interested in the "good girl" O-Tane himself. First-person narration gives us a special key to the narrator's thoughts. On the other hand, a first-person narrator's limited knowledge of the thoughts and actions of other characters can make them seem remote or their motives unfathomable, especially in comparison with the intimate view we have of the narrator.

However, we feel we understand Egawa and the "other woman," O-Tama, because of what they reveal about themselves in conversation with the narrator. When there is only time to draw a character with a few quick strokes, the result can be as much caricature as characterization. Hakuchō avoids caricature more successfully in "Suffocation" than in such earlier stories as "Ghost Picture," "Whither?", and "Wasted Effort."

Successful characterization of the minor characters aids that of the narrator. He acquires a social dimension; we know that he is dealing with other people, not shadows or aspects of his imagination. That is the contribution of dialogue. For example, early in the story the narrator meets with O-Tama and then goes to a storyteller's hall (*yose*) rather than visit O-Tane and her family. On the way home he decides to visit his friend Egawa. Egawa, as it turns out, has met O-Tane and her family for the first time that night in the course of looking for the young narrator.

"I went to your place tonight, but you weren't home. I thought you were probably at O-Tane's house, so I went there. They were all wondering why you didn't come. Her mother was worried that you might have found some nice place to amuse yourself." Egawa said with a serious look.

"I had some business," I said evasively. "But I don't go there that often anyway," I then explained.

"But they have such a pleasant family — hospitable![26] Considering their sophistication, they're all delightfully unaffected. I think I'll go visit them sometimes from now on." He gazed calmly at me; he spoke in his characteristically abrupt manner. "They seem to regard you as one of the family. And, they're overestimating you a bit." He smiled faintly; he sounded sarcastic to me.

"They're not especially overestimating me, because I'm completely honest with them."

"But both men and women overestimate the people they like."

Egawa left his chair and sat cross-legged on the tatami. He smoked a cigarette. Moonlight flowed in beneath the shallow eaves; the lamp flame flickered in the cool breeze. I felt pity for the dark-complected fellow I saw, with his excessive philosophizing and shutting himself up in his cramped room.

"They really trust you too much over there." Egawa said almost as an afterthought, and again produced his faint smile.

"It's only natural," I said proudly. "I've got a likable nature. Never in my life has anyone particularly disliked me. I even think I'd like to be thoroughly disliked once to see how it feels."

"That's because you've never noticed it yourself. But you'll be lucky if you can go through your whole life with that attitude. Because deep down inside people are always honing the edge of their hatred for one another. You don't understand because you're still inexperienced, but I've had terrible experiences long ago, so I know all too well." (*MHZ*, I, 470–471)

Egawa goes on to describe how he was once bitterly deceived by the woman he loved, but just the above reveals much of his character. He is bitter, egotistical, and opportunistic. But he is also a clear-sighted realist who can see that O-Tane and her family are making too much of the narrator. We see Egawa only through the narrator's eyes, but there is no indication that Hakuchō has the naive young man subjectively distorting the substance of the dialogue.

The young narrator's makeup is brought into better focus through his interaction with such a character as Egawa. He is deceptive and self-centered, but possesses a naive optimism which contrasts with Egawa's pessimism born of disappointment.

For Hakuchō's fiction the above quotation is relatively fast-paced. When the narrator paraphrases and summarizes, rather than delineates, his dealings with other people, the story seems slower and ineffective. Hakuchō's fiction would have benefited from more use of dialogue, even in "Suffocation." As it is, the story must remain that of the young narrator.

Here Hakuchō succeeds for the most part, since the young man is believable. He is young; he has just graduated from college and has little experience. He is sensual, emotional, and impulsive — all of which seems believable, especially when he is describing O-Tane, for example, in sudoriferous detail. The story takes place during the heat of summer; in the following he is a guest of O-Tane one sultry afternoon:

The sun grew increasingly stronger. It seemed scorching as it shone down on the garden. The wind had died; not a tree leaf stirred. There were blotches of sweat even on O-Tane's face. "It's so hot!" she sighed again and again with a frown. I couldn't help but imagine her smooth skin moist with sweat. There was the pungent smell of perspiration and her hair in the sultry air.

I didn't want to go out into the heat outdoors, so I welcomed their detaining me. I was even invited to dinner, so I lingered until nightfall. It was unusual to spend a day like that. Mother and daughter were getting up and sitting down, moving all about the house taking care of various household errands. Alertly my eyes followed every movement of O-Tane's sweat-covered body. The bottoms of her feet when she stretched her body and stood on tiptoe, the view of her from behind when she bent over ... I had seen her before in light make-up, dressed up, and playing the koto, but the sight of O-Tane unmade up as she was that day excited me much more. (*MHZ*, I, 473–474)

This is truly description of physical detail. The selection of details and emphasis on animal physicality indicates an attitude probably hard to find in serious Meiji fiction before the Naturalist years. Compared to most of Hakuchō's other stories, "Suffocation" abounds in such scenes.

Despite the detail, the description of O-Tane is totally a product of the narrator's recollections. O-Tane speaks very little in "Suffocation," and perhaps as a result she remains a two-dimensional character. We know her effect upon the narrator, but never who she really is.

The fact that the young narrator has cut himself off from his family's advice by remaining in Tokyo — rather than coming home to spend the summer after graduation — allows him to make his own decisions. Being the type of young person he is, he follows passion or whim rather than common sense. When he begins to feel caught between the two women, he purchases a knife. The knife gives him a new and sudden sense of security; we are immediately anxious that Hakuchō will resolve his story through a violent rage of impotence. That would have been a mistake, for although the narrator is impulsive and somewhat isolated, there is little to indicate such intensity or psychosis.

The purchase of the knife itself seems the limit of his youthful impetuosity. There is the possibility of tragedy in his future, assuming his choice of the disreputable O-Tama will lead to a further remove from respectable society. A sense of opportunities lost, which he clearly expresses, may someday outreach the consolations of his final attitude of resignation, especially when he loses his youthful fire. We are certainly aware of this as the story closes, but it is still a young man's story. Although we may see the young man's choice of O-Tama as a shame, it is no tragedy.

The Meiji *kabuki* classic *Botan dōrō* (The Peony Lantern) is mentioned at several points in "Suffocation." Hakuchō was fond of *kabuki,* as we have seen, and of such popular forms of entertainment as storytelling (*rakugo* or *yose*). The narrator of "Suffocation" frequently visits storyteller's halls to hear *The Peony Lantern,* in which the ghost of the woman O-Tsuyu, after many suspense-building attempts, finally succeeds in claiming her terrified former lover, Hagiwara Shinzaburō, to carry him off to the other realm.

When O-Tama is solidifying her hold upon the narrator, he has a dream in which she is the ghost from *The Peony Lantern* and he is bound and unable to escape her (*MHZ*, I, 489). He later reasons that he is indeed the type of man women cannot forget, just like Shinzaburō. O-Tama is truly his O-Tsuyu. He feels there is something inexplicable about the curse put on unforgettable types like himself and Shinzaburō (*MHZ,* I, 492).

When the narrator's predicament is expressed in such terms, it becomes difficult to take him too seriously. Just as the chill of the frightening *Peony Lantern* cools the summer theater patron, perhaps writing "Suffocation" in the summer of 1911 helped Hakuchō forget the frustrations of his marriage that April.

CHAPTER 4

Other Stories

I *"By the Inlet" (1915)*

B Y the Inlet" (April, 1915) is an early example of a style of writing Hakuchō would frequently rely upon for the remainder of his career. Such stories were autobiographical, highly factual works with the identities of the actual persons disguised, often but thinly. Hakuchō is nearly always one of the characters, but often, as in "By the Inlet," he is not the focus of the story.

Characteristically, these stories are portraits of Hakuchō's family members. Many of the pieces Japanese commentators find among his most memorable stories — "Autumn of This Year" (1959), for example — are of this type. They may appear objective in their view of their material, but invariably contain a subjective note as well. Even those in the form of a third-person omniscient narrative seem somehow imbued with a first-person perception.

The model for Tatsuo, the "hero" of "By the Inlet," is the fourth of the six Masamune sons to survive childhood — Ritsushi. Along with the later portrait of his father, he is one of the more unforgettable characters Hakuchō "created." The depth of the impression made by a writer's characters is one measure of his achievement. Hakuchō's success in that area is with Ono of "Dust," Kenji of "Whither?", Sōkichi of "Wasted Effort," and the fictionalizations of his father and brother Ritsushi.

The story takes place in a small village on the Inland Sea, obviously Hakuchō's own Honami. The many brothers and sisters are mostly in their twenties or early thirties. The eldest brother Eiichi (Hakuchō) is well established in Tokyo. As the story opens, they are looking forward to his first visit home in several years.

Eiichi disappoints them first by postponing his arrival and then by arriving in the middle of the night. One brother has left for

Tokyo before Eiichi arrives; a younger sister, Katsuyo, is planning her own trip to Tokyo to study and talks of nothing else. They are all either trying to get ahead in business at home or dreaming the provincial's dream of going to Tokyo for education and excitement.

Only Tatsuo differs from the others. He is nearly thirty, and withdrawn almost to the point of psychosis. Somehow he functions as an English teacher at a local school, although he has no teaching credentials, is self-taught, and not too knowledgeable in English. He has his own idiosyncratic conception of English; he spends most of his time alone at his desk in his second-floor room that looks out on the inlet, writing inferior English compositions that have meaning mostly for just himself.

Once his sister, who is sleeping nearby, awakes in pain in the middle of the night. She is suffering greatly and calls out for help, for someone — Tatsuo — to bring her medicine. Tatsuo, however, quietly moves his bedding to where he can no longer hear her. On another occasion, Tatsuo accidentally starts a fire in his room. After it is put out, he will give his disquieted relatives no explanation of how the fire began. He then insists on sleeping that night in the charred room, rather than in the same room with Eiichi.

The contrast between the two brothers, the articulate Eiichi and the taciturn Tatsuo, is seen when they hike up the mountain overlooking the inlet together. Eiichi has asked Tatsuo what purpose he has in studying English, but he remains silent, watching the flight of a blackbird while trying to think of the English word for "fly." Eiichi must again question him:

"Are you studying to pass the examination for a teacher's certificate or do you just find English interesting?"

"I wouldn't say it's dull," Tatsuo replied at last evasively, although he himself had never felt that it was particularly interesting or uninteresting.

"No matter how many years you study, you won't be able to get a teacher's certificate if you study on your own. Language study is different from other subjects. It's no use unless you practice a little with a teacher."

". . . ." Tatsuo kept silent and lowered his eyes.

"Better yet, perhaps you should use that time to study the subjects for the elementary school teacher's examination and hurry up and qualify yourself as a regular teacher. Your paltry salary is intolerable for a man nearly thirty years old."

" . . . . " The dead oak leaves being turned over at his feet by the wind caught Tatsuo's eye. He felt an unpleasant dreariness.

"Recently I've gotten a look at the English compositions you wrote. They're completely confused and totally incomprehensible. They amount to no more than stringing a lot of words together. To devote yourself to that kind of thing for four or five years is the height of absurdity. Your pronunciation must be all the more riddled with mistakes. It's no good to rely upon writing in the pronunciation in Japanese to give you a clue."

" . . . . "

"If you're doing it for amusement, anything will do. Still something like *waka* or haiku you can do even in the country. Even if you are bad at it, you can still show them to people, which should make it more interesting, shouldn't it? I don't see any point in making English compositions that no one can understand. Did you really intend them to communicate to other people?"

Eiichi had spoken sharply. Rather than pity for his younger brother's foolishness, his tone seemed to deride and abuse him.

" . . . . " Tatsuo shut his dark lips tightly, and tears rose to his eyes. Of course he was neither reading to teach others nor writing compositions to show others. He had known all along that his English was not precise, but to have his older brother decide that it was completely worthless seemed utterly heartless.

"Well, shall we go?" Eiichi said and he brushed the dust from his clothes and headed back down the path. (*MHZ,* II, 246)

We see that "By the Inlet" contains an objective, impersonal characterization of the cold, intelligent Eiichi, but is subjective — or "sweet," to borrow the Japanese term *amai* — in describing the lonely, helpless Tatsuo. This implies a change in Hakuchō's relation to his material. He will increasingly reveal his feelings about the real-life events and characters he re-creates in his writing. This calls to mind a similar change another Naturalist writer, Tokuda Shūsei, underwent during the Taishō years.

During the 1910s and 1920s Hakuchō seemed to retreat from the Naturalist ideal of total detachment and objectivity. From "By the Inlet" even to the time of "Autumn of This Year" and "Elder Brother Rii" (1961) Hakuchō relied heavily, though by no means exclusively, on such stories. Hakuchō continued to employ a realistic method — faithful descriptions of objective reality, willingness to include mundane subject matter. However, value judgments and personal observations that would be rejected by a Naturalist were now often made either directly or by implication.

II   *"Until He Takes the Sleeping Medicine" (1916)*
and "The Dead and the Living" (1916)

In 1916 Hakuchō produced three stories that further illustrate
the process of his stylistic development. They were: "Until He
Takes the Sleeping Medicine," January; "The Smell of the Cowshed," May; and "The Dead and the Living," September. All three
appeared in *Chūō Kōron.*[1] The differences between these works
show Hakuchō did not restrict himself to any one type of story.

"Until He Takes the Sleeping Medicine" continues Hakuchō's
earlier successful vein of accounts of the misunderstood literatus-
as-a-young-man. However, the hero Sukejirō seems less convincing
than those of "Whither?" and "Clay Doll." "Sleeping Medicine"
is an account of domestic psychological tension in a quarrelsome
household containing Sukejirō, female cousins, his hardhearted
older brother, and his beautiful wife O-Sugi.

Sukejirō is of marriageable age and longs for female companionship. He is attracted to his sister-in-law and she figures in his sexual
fantasies. However, the sophisticated O-Sugi enjoys teasing Sukejirō and takes him no more seriously than she does anyone else. The
story concludes with the troubled young man — he has headaches
— apparently taking an overdose of sleeping medicine and lying
down with the feeling he's being led to some "bright, beautiful
place" (*MHZ,* II, 296).

The notion of the family as thwarting individual happiness is of
note; the father and eldest son dominate and control everything,
especially money. Sister-in-law O-Sugi shares in this domination.
She is a type of female character Hakuchō often created. She has a
strong, animal personality, and easily controls the other family
members through her strength (the women) or more successfully
through her feminine charm (the men).

The failure of "Sleeping Medicine" is the unconvincing "hero";
his final action, in particular, seems inexplicable. Perhaps, Hakuchō had outgrown this theme of the troubled young man so that he
could no longer inject vitality into such characterizations.

In "The Dead and the Living" Hakuchō treats members of the
working class, petty shopkeepers. This was a favorite sector of
society of the Western Naturalist. In Japan, Tokuda Shūsei began
his Naturalist fiction with "A New Household" (*Arajotai*) (1908),
which also deals with a young shopkeeper.

Both "A New Household" and "The Dead and the Living" contain a love triangle. In Shūsei's story an attractive interloper tries unsuccessfully to win the young shopkeeper away from his homely bride. The drama is thoroughly domestic, the characters are true proletarians, and the result is a primer of realistic style and Naturalistic outlook.

In Hakuchō's story, however, although the narrative is similarly precise and photographic, additional philosophical elements are present. The shopkeeper in "The Dead and The Living" is dying. His wife nurses him out of a sense of duty, but her affections have been transferred to a hard-working young man recently brought into the household to help with the store.

The husband only partially senses the extent of the threat of the intrusion of the younger man, for the dying man is preoccupied with his own spiritual salvation. He convinces his wife to have his head shaved, despite her embarrassed reluctance. She fears the ridicule of the neighbors when they see such an extreme display of religious piety. The husband has no fear of such ridicule and even wants his wife to have her head shaved, too, so that she may join him in Buddhist prayer for his salvation.

The description of the man's "tonsure" is a moving sequence in the midst of an otherwise gray story.

> The cold touch of the clippers on the skin of his head felt good. As the sick man watched his long hair fall in front of him, he felt as if he were being shown palpably the anguish of his long illness, and he wept. (*MHZ*, II, 344)

The younger man watches silently and the wife is only able to attempt light-hearted, mindless comments. But, for the first time, the sick man is able to recite the *"nembutsu"* (a prayer to Amida Buddha) not to relieve his pain, but "from the heart" (*MHZ*, II, 344).

Hakuchō does not describe the actual death of the shopkeeper. As a sort of a postscript he brings us up to date, noting that in the spring the husband's name on the store sign was replaced by the young man's. The sign on the store bicycle was similarly changed in the fall, the maid now sleeps alone downstairs, and so on.

To Shūsei's story a postscript is added telling that the shopkeeper is celebrating the third anniversary of the opening of his store and that his wife is pregnant again. In both stories life goes on and belongs to the living in "The Dead and The Living" and to the triumphant in "A New Household." The difference is the lingering image of the dead man's religious ecstasy in the Hakuchō story.

Shūsei is generally acknowledged as the best writer, or storyteller, among the Naturalists, with the probable exception of Shimazaki Tōson. But, lacking Hakuchō's insistent spirit of philosophical inquiry, he was incapable of such a dramatic, almost Tolstoyean moment. Ōiwa Kō feels that the end of the predominance in Hakuchō's stories of "Realism" — he borrows the English — occurs at about the time of "The Dead and the Living."[2]

But "The Dead and the Living" is just further evidence of what we have noted of Hakuchō's "Naturalistic" stories such as "Whither?", "Hell," and "Wasted Effort." A clearly religious and characteristically Hakuchōean element can often exist even in his gloomiest, most nihilistic stories.

III   *"The Smell of the Cowshed" (1916)*

"The Smell of the Cowshed" concerns the woman Kikuyo, her aged and infirm grandmother, and blind mother, all of whom live in hopeless poverty in a foul and drafty building that had originally been used to house animals. The three women offer definite contrasts to one another in the philosophies they develop to accept the misery of their lives.

The old grandmother has no spirituality at all; she is a true animal. All her life she has lived only for sensual gratification. At this stage of her life she thinks only of food and drink. She is ostensibly the closest to death, but the thought of her death never crosses her mind. Kikuyo's older sister had been forced into prostitution; she went off to a distant city and has not been heard from in years. Nevertheless, the old woman wants to sell her other granddaughter, Kikuyo, into prostitution, for she is convinced she then would be well off from her earnings.

Kikuyo's mother, O-Natsu, is the opposite of the old woman. She has two dreams: that her older daughter is still alive and will one day come sailing back to their fishing village; and that she herself can someday make a pilgrimage to the temple of Konpira[3] on the island of Shikoku. O-Natsu, despite her blindness, runs errands for the other villagers; she does so happily, thinking that the small coins she receives can be saved toward her pilgrimage or given to her unhappy daughter, Kikuyo.

Kikuyo is the saddest of the three. She is incapable of losing herself in religious devotion like her mother, but also too intelligent to be insensitive, like her grandmother, to the humiliation of life in the village. Kikuyo's first husband was shot as an army deserter; her second husband ran off to Korea several years before. Kikuyo manages a meager income through itinerant peddling of dry fruit and other things.

The time of the story is the lunar New Year. The drab poverty of the lives of the three women makes it impossible for them to join in the boisterous celebrations of the other villagers. However, in the midst of the holiday Kikuyo's husband, who has been in prison, returns unexpectedly. She is hostile toward him at first, but, out of the desperation of her loneliness, finally agrees to renew their relationship. Because he used to beat both of the older women, he is not welcome in the cowshed. They meet at a fishing boat aboard which a friend is letting him sleep.

They drink *sake* and eat fish alone on the ship and Kikuyo cannot believe her surprising good fortune. But when the drunken owner of the boat suddenly returns, she hides below. From her hiding place, she hears the man urge her husband to take her back, reasoning that with such an ugly beggar for a wife he need never worry about her deceiving him with another man when he is out to sea. What other man would have her?

When the man leaves, Kikuyo becomes frantic in her humiliation. She wants to steal the boat and run away from the village. Her husband explains the impossibility of escaping without money. She vows to steal some. She hurries along the night streets toward a rich storehouse; every villager she encounters along the way she regards as her enemy. She hides herself near the storehouse, but ironically her mother has heard someone enter the yard and alerts a maid. The owner of the storehouse thus discovers Kikuyo there; he cannot accuse her of theft but he is suspicious. O-Natsu leads Kikuyo home, where the old woman tries to console her by suggesting they invite her husband over for a drink the next day.

Striking is the character of the mother, O-Natsu. She is as symbolic as any character in Hakuchō's literature of the "blind faith" he admired in "On Dante." She is literally blind and the only one of the women who believes in the efficacy of offerings to Buddhist or Shinto deities.

The old grandmother is at times humorous, but also at times disgusting. O-Natsu points out specifically that the old woman will not pray to Buddha even now that she is crippled and near death.

She wants only another cup of *sake* or another discarded fishhead. Spiritually, she has learned nothing from her long, difficult life. Still, Hakuchō gives a sympathetic twist to her characterization when at the end she is able to offer some sympathy to Kikuyo, although even then it is mixed with self-interest.

Kikuyo sacrifices her life out of a sense of duty. She cannot run off and start life anew — which seems to have been definitely impossible — for she must take care of the old women. She endures poverty for them, but the accumulation of humiliation and degradation, symbolized by the odor and discomfort of the cowshed, creates an unbearable psychological tension. The paranoia she exhibits in the final scene has its origin in the ridicule she overhears in the boat. It confirms an image of herself she was undoubtedly aware of, but unable to acknowledge and accept consciously.

Kikuyo knows she and her family are the lowest members of the village social unit, that they are obvious objects of scorn, but she must flee from an acceptance of this self-image. Her aborted escape attempt seems an act of madness in its desperation, but, in fact, it is brought about by a moment of clarity. That is, Kikuyo suddenly sees things as they really are; all of her psychological defenses are shoved aside by the experience on the boat, which comes as a final, devastating blow in a life of enduring pain.

O-Natsu also consoles herself with illusions. She accepts the present reality, but has mystic hopes for the future. Her future happiness is tied to the return of her oldest daughter. These illusions are shattered in the final scene, for she has a premonition of her eldest daughter's death.

Kikuyo loses her illusions about the present, her mother her illusions about the future. It is the blind mother who leads her daughter home to safety, however. She is the only one who sees, or understands, the present; she is the one who is frightened at the thought of how Kikuyo's new state of mind will affect their lives. O-Natsu is the one who understands the present and so knows intuitively, as Hakuchō himself did intellectually, the need for religious or mystic "illusions" about the future to make the present bearable.

Although Hakuchō wrote "The Smell of the Cowshed" several years after what is usually considered the end of the Naturalist era in Japan, it is in this story that Hakuchō seems the closest to the spirit of the Western Naturalist writer. The ramshackle building that inspired the story was still standing near the Masamune household in Honami as late as the 1960s; the model for the heroine was living in an old people's home.⁴ From his room Hakuchō could hear the conversation from their "house"; from all evidence it appears that he used their actual conversation exactly as he heard it.⁵

Depiction of such destitution and squalor was typical of Western Naturalists. They found the poor and unfortunate much better subjects for illustrating man's animal nature and the fight for survival than the wealthy and leisured who seem to defy natural laws.

Given the wealth of the Masamune family, Hakuchō could have built these unfortunate people a house or helped them in some way, had he so chosen; the son of the blind lady lived in the shed until the roof collapsed in 1964.⁶ Actual intervention in their lives would have been too much to expect of him, for his relation to the reality of their squalid existence is, like that of most Western Naturalists to their material, merely that of an observer. Hakuchō's attitude in "Cowshed" is much like that of Western Naturalists, the scientists of novelists, observing life and noting the details so that they may re-create reality in their art. Only in this frozen form is a reality as stark as that of the people in the cowshed approachable.

Hakuchō's instinctive interest in such unfortunate people as his lonely brother in "By the Inlet" and the women in the shed shows his innate sensitivity to the suffering of others. Something in his retiring personality, or perhaps even in his nature as a Japanese conditioned toward noninvolvement, prevented him from reaching out to such people. Still, there seems to be a contradiction between what we might conveniently call his Asian fatalism, seeing the plight of his brother Rii and the people in the cowshed as inevitable, and the dictates of the alien religion, Christianity, which warns "Though I speak with the tongues of men and of angels, and have not charity, I am become as sounding brass, or a tinkling cymbal."⁷

IV   *"Nightmare" (1921) and "Various People" (1921)*

Thematically, Hakuchō's stories are, for the most part, of two types. One deals with such themes as insanity, murder, and fantasy; the other is characterized by depiction of ordinary life. Both types of stories are permeated with Hakuchō's overriding philosophical concerns. "Nightmare" (January, 1921) and "Various People" (September, 1921) illustrate this duality.

"Nightmare" concerns a love triangle consisting of a physician,

Toyomura, his wife Kayoko, and his mistress Tomoe. However, the theme of the story is not love but the relativity of reality, that is, a discussion of how the reality of the senses relates to that of the imagination.

Toyomura and Tomoe are on one of their secret weekends in Ōiso, where they engage in philosophical conversations both in their hotel room and along the beach. Toyomura is unusually serious and talks of making their relationship permanent.

Tomoe is not interested in marriage; she wants to live totally in the present with no thought of the future. As they gaze at the endless sea, both agree that experiencing the reality of each moment directly is superior to experiencing reality indirectly by glimpsing its reflections on stage or film. In that case, says Tomoe, they should forget the complications of their lives in Tokyo until they return there the next day.

Tomoe runs barefoot on the beach; this entices even the cynical, blasé Toyomura to run barefoot with her. She says as long as she is young and healthy, she has no need of gloomy preoccupations. She often wonders, she says, why people do not delight in the beauty of their bodies, why man devised clothing, why people cannot enjoy the things they like in the company they choose without worrying about the restrictions of family and society. She wishes she could run naked in the sand; she is drawn, irresistibly, to the sea.

Toyomura is reminded of the poetry of Byron and Coleridge. And he is drawn to the sea, too. They gaze out to sea together and find that they are both struck by the same thoughts of how they would like to sail far away. She exclaims,

"You and I were both thinking of the same thing!"

"But there's no use thinking about the impossible."

"Why? It's not impossible. I think we could do it tomorrow, or even today, if we really wanted to. Maybe it's because you're intelligent and know everything, but it seems a man like you is incapable of daring action. I don't think I can rely on a man who calls his own ideas foolish."

She was without her usual innocence as she spoke; her words struck Toyomura as chilling. Perhaps it was his imagination, but her look was glaring and without its accustomed innocent gentleness. Toyomura was forced to look away. (*MHZ*, III, 12–13)

Back in their hotel room, Toyomura curls up like a child listening to a fairy tale as Tomoe tells him her version of the story of Adam and Eve: Adam and Eve had lived in ignorant, naked bliss in Paradise. If only they had been satisfied with its pleasures, but each came to have secret yearnings. Eve saw clouds in the shape of a man; Adam left the sleeping Eve and tried to walk to where the stars seemed brighter, only to find they shone the same no matter where he went.

Eve began to notice that something was distracting Adam and eventually confronted him with questions. She was mild at first but finally became acrimonious. Once the doubts were unleashed, they grew and came between them, destroying their former intimacy. Adam longed to know Eve's secret thoughts. Obsessed, he split her open but found nothing within her breast he had not known before. All that he accomplished was her death. Strangely, with death her face reassumed its former gentleness and beauty.

The pleasures of Paradise were there for Adam as before, but he could not live on in Paradise without Eve. He buried her and left the garden. He wandered off into the cold and darkness.

The bliss of the weekend rendezvous, also, is interrupted when the arrival of Toyomura's wife Kayoko is announced. Toyomura has the clerk tell Kayoko he is not at the hotel and the clerk later reports that Kayoko left quietly.

Toyomura returns immediately to his home in Tokyo; he is apprehensive about the emotional scene that will surely ensue. His wife returns later than he; she gives no indication that she has been to Ōiso. She claims that she has been merely to the theater, although it afforded her no relaxation. Of late, she says, she has been possessed by a vengeful spirit (*onryō*); it gives her no peace and makes her clearly aware of her husband's every thought and deed.

He tries to ascribe to her nerves her feeling that she is possessed by a vengeful spirit, but we know that while in Ōiso he himself had had vivid thoughts of *The Peony Lantern* which he had seen once with Tomoe. The murder of the man by the possessive, vengeful spirit of the woman was especially clear in his thoughts. Kayoko looks to him as if indeed she is possessed by such a vengeful spirit, so that he must avert his eyes.

They quarrel and he suggests they separate, which calls forth an angry outburst.

"So you say separate. That would be most convenient for you." There was a frightening gleam in Kayoko's eyes. "I know all about the promises you made with that woman in Ōiso!"

_ Toyomura had been on edge for some time; when he heard the word Oiso from Kayoko's lips, he felt all the blood in his body go to his head. It was as if he were having a nightmare. He felt as if the vengeful spirit of this woman had stolen away from her theater seat and gone to the beach at Ōiso. "How long do you intend to haunt me?" he shouted and immediately lept at her; in a daze, he choked her slender neck.

His frail wife did not utter a sound; as she clung to her husband's hands, her breathing stopped and she turned up the whites of her eyes.

Toyomura was like a madman as he stood gazing at the figure of the dead woman. Finally he came to himself, and, as if it were expected of him as a physician, took her in his arms and checked her body warmth and pulse. It seemed to him that with a little treatment she could be saved.

But, although he realized she could be saved, he thought unpleasantly of the aftermath of bringing Kayoko back to life and allowed himself a moment's hesitation.

How difficult her life would be after this point, and his own life thus disrupted, for a brief moment, these thoughts played a distinct and active part in his mind. (*MHZ,* III, 27)

Hakuchō is playing with the theme of vengeful spirits, which is hardly the stuff of realistic fiction. Hakuchō's fascination with murder, in this case strangulation, is seen again. Its effectiveness is diminished by the absence of any previous indication of Toyomura's capacity for violence.

Having Toyomura waver between saving and killing his wife is the kind of literary artifice for which Hakuchō at times criticized other writers, such as Sōseki. He is, of course, trying to dramatize Toyomura's dilemma which has its source in his negative view of life. That view of life seems determined by his negative view of himself. Married to him, a worthless cad by his own admission, his wife will see only continued sorrow, so let her die for her own good.

Toyomura easily ignores the immorality of taking another's life; it is frequently stated that he regards women as simply creatures or animals. His willingness to murder is believable, which compensates somewhat for the unlikelihood of such a violent rage in an otherwise placid character.

As in some other similar Hakuchō works — "Discord and Harmony," "The Joys of Life" — it is the slightly mysterious, ethereal nature of a female character, Tomoe, that is the most intriguing aspect of the story. Her philosophy of living for the present is deliberately associated with youth and its "illusions." For example, her older lover is aware of the complications of society and the brevity of life, so that he is often troubled in his sleep. The young girl, however, usually sleeps soundly and much later than he.

The "nightmare" of the final scene is the horror of being confronted with the complexity of the truth. This is the moment of reality for the married couple as they drop pretense and acknowledge the facts they have been aware of secretly all along. The horror of the truth brought to light surpasses any of the bizarre fantasies dredged up from the darkness of the subconscious on a sleepless night.

Such is the lesson of Tomoe's parable of Adam and Eve. Paradise was to be enjoyed in a continuum of present moments. There is, in Tomoe's view, no other reality than that of the present moment and concrete, objective reality. But, like Toyomura, Adam could not be content with only that which his senses perceived. Something within him makes him aware of mystery, of the presence of the supernatural. He sought it first in the dark reaches of space and then within Eve. He destroyed the present by not accepting it simply as it was.

Likewise, Toyomura talks to Tomoe of marriage, that is, of future happiness, although Tomoe is his own Eve and the beach and hotels of Ōiso his own Paradise if he will only accept them. In this notion of man's unshakeable awareness of a realm beyond that of the purely natural destroying his equilibrium, "Nightmare" shares a thematic bond with the later "Illusion." The impossibility of philosophical peace owing to a persistent, gnawing preoccupation with the improbable existence of the supernatural is the central theme, the heart, of Hakuchō's writing.

This thematic core is apparent even in a work of a vastly different style than "Nightmare" — "Various People." It is a highly autobiographical account of the wanderings of Hakuchō and his wife Tsune after their return from Honami in May, 1920. Hakuchō and Tsune are Mr. and Mrs. Takayama in "Various People."

The Takayamas are well off financially, but the leisure of their lives is tinged with boredom and gloom. Takayama recognizes that much of his ennui stems directly from his leisure. Much of his gloom is the result of his constant awareness of the transiency of human life.

Mrs. Takayama wants more stability and security in their lives. She cannot understand her husband who daydreams of living many years abroad, preferably in the remotest places he can imagine, such as Persia or Turkey. When he relates such daydreams, she simply wonders what would become of her if he really did go off to Persia.

What he does not relate to his wife are the fears that beset him on sleepless nights, fears of growing old, feeble, senile, thoughts that lead invariably to viewing suicide as a rational resolution. In contrast to these thoughts of self-destruction are persistent longings for deliverance of a different nature. He is attracted to aspects of both Buddhism and Christianity. Whereas his wife desires possessions and financial security, he views their unsettled state as an opportunity to achieve more simplicity in their lives by rejecting material possessions. Pressure from his wife and many in-laws makes this difficult, however.

As for Christianity, in the midst of his boredom Takayama thinks of visiting a priest he had once known, who has been running an orphanage in Kyushu for the past twenty years. Hakuchō conceives of two paths leading away from his dissatisfying idleness: one is Christianity, for example, a life devoted to doing good works; the other alternative is resolution through a violent act of catharsis, usually murder. The latter we have seen in "Nightmare." The two are equated in "Various People" as Takayama thinks of the priest in Kyushu.

Attending to the education of the unfortunate little children in that remote place is the noblest life a man can lead. The ladder that links this world with Heaven may stand in such a place. But when he considered the possibility of following such a pastor and working contentedly himself, the mere thought of it was ridiculous.
(If I cannot find peace of mind by murdering someone, I won't be able to find it by helping others. Either course amounts to the same thing.) (*MHZ*, III, 47)

The choice in Hakuchō's life was always between faith and desperation. Personally following either course was for most of his life impossible for Hakuchō. The role of his writing was to articulate and clarify such a view. In "Various People," Takayama at one point loses himself in his writing for days. His total absorption in this furious writing bout provides his only escape from his usual boredom and morbidity. Hakuchō's writing functioned primarily as a tool for shaping his philosophy which always wavered between hope and despair.

V   *"Illusion" (1922)*

The imagery of "Illusion" (May, 1922) is drawn from disparate sources: Greek mythology, the Bible, Japanese folklore, Chinese Taoist poetry, Dante, Japanese poetry, and the writing of Mori Ōgai. As in no other story Hakuchō creates a self-contained, symbolic drama whose symbiotic elements suggest the complex eclecticism of his intellect. Hakuchō's intellectual complexity must account for much of the high regard of his contemporaries. The uniqueness of "Illusion" is apparent from its opening lines.

One night a toad began to croak by an old pond. It seemed to announce the coming of spring, but after a few days it stopped. When the hermit went to look, at the water's edge he found countless squirming, spotted, serpentine objects.

He thought, unpleasantly, that they must be frog's eggs. He lifted them with a stick and exposed them to the spring sunlight. There were black grains encased in a gelatinous membrane. One by one the black grains would develop into tadpoles. At length they would acquire the bodies of frogs and crawl up onto the land. If left alone, how many tens of thousands of frogs would appear? He was reminded of the congratulatory words of the foreign God, "Be fruitful and multiply, and fill the waters in the seas."[8]

The hermit was afraid both his garden and all the area about his lonely old thatched hut would become home for the frogs. He thought of clubbing them to death in their eggs, but he had no need to kill them himself. The stray cat that sometimes appeared could reach them from the bank, or jump from rock to rock, rake together the frog's eggs and devour them. They multiply and are destroyed. The hermit could not divine the feelings of the alien God Who created living beings so that they went on living by destroying others. (*MHZ*, III, 102)

The hermit spends his days observing, reading, meditating. His inability to find spiritual peace is contrasted with the detachment of a poem by the T'ang dynasty Taoist Han Shan:

> If you're looking for a place to rest,
> Cold Mountain is good for a long stay.
> The breeze blowing through the dark pines
> Sounds better the closer you come.
> And under the trees a white-haired man
> Mumbles over his Taoist texts.
> Ten years now he hasn't gone home;
> He's even forgotten the road he came by.[9]

The hermit lives in a world inhabited by characters from the philosophical and literary traditions of both the East and the West.

The hermit is visited by three spirits (*mōryō*). The first one is very solemn in appearance and advises the hermit to seek that sixth sense with which all great men — poets, saints, even scientists — have "seen into the secrets of the universe and the depths of the human spirit" (*MHZ,* III, 103).

The hermit acknowledges the existence of this sense, but adds:

"...a man learns so little through his five senses. I doubt that a man can become an omniscient god by the addition of just one more different sense. A sixth sense might be of use for meaningless display, but even if people appeared with not just a sixth sense, but a seventh or eighth, it would be no reason for me to revere them especially. They will perish like the grass in the fields, or the frogs and earthworms. The more extraordinary their senses, the more I pity them." (*MHZ,* III, 103)

The first spirit concludes that it is useless to argue with the hermit and disappears. Soon an oddly shaped spirit appears. His shape is that of a prickly tree with dark leaves and gnarled branches. In the trunk of the tree is a mouth, like that of a human, through which he speaks.

"I was cast in this wretched form hundreds of years ago by a temperamental poet. As retribution for suicide, we are turned into trees, bereft of reason. Soul and body are to be separate forever. Our bowels are food for the foul beasts that nest in our hair. I hear it is commanded that for eternity, those who've ended their own lives can never return their souls to their bodies. I've borne my anguish for centuries. (*MHZ,* III, 104)

He goes on to bemoan the cruelty of the "God, Jehovah" and the poet, obviously Dante, who was "His tool." The spirit had committed suicide not to escape any earthly problems, but in the belief that with the death of the body, the spirit dies, too. He says: "I was like Mainlaender,[10] who killed himself in his youth, believing death superior to life" (*MHZ,* III, 104). He now knows how mistaken that was, and eternal suffering in this wretched form is his punishment.

The spirit warns the hermit of the dangers of the immortal soul, to which the hermit replies:

"If you can't destroy your own soul, even if you try, then is there probably no way to obtain peace? Is the wisest course to follow God blindly and beg His mercy?"

The hermit inquired without much enthusiasm, however. His head pecked by beasts, his expression pained, the apparition seemed to groan as he replied.

"People have been consoled by the thought of it for ages, but does that mean you, also, believe in the existence of divine mercy? Do you think there is any mercy in the God Who tortures us and won't even grant us a second death?" (*MHZ*, III, 105)

This second spirit also disappears; the hermit is stunned by his speech and examines listlessly the vivid descriptions of the suffering of the damned in the works of "the poet."

Finally, a third spirit appears who looks exactly like the hermit himself. He urges the hermit to ignore thoughts of heaven and hell, which, he says, exist only in man's imagination. This third spirit explains that only what man perceives with his eyes and ears is real. He disappears when the hermit angrily tells him that he does not need to be told that there is no immortal soul, that desires are inevitable in man but vanish with death.

The spirit who looked like the hermit reappeared, but red in color, like flames.

"You're trembling at the sounds from the village, but do you know what has happened there?"

"I don't think I want to know. Even if they've begun killing one another or they're having an earthquake, that has little to do with me. There's absolutely no connection between what I devote my thoughts to and what happens in the village. I intend to treat my books, apparitions like yourself, and living human beings all the same."

"You may say that while you can, but the time has come for you to decide right away. Do you or don't you desire the extinction of your soul?"

The spirit who looked like him was insistent. Ordered to decide, the hermit felt himself being strangled. The spirit pressing him for a reply, also, seemed to be in pain as if he, too, were being strangled.

No matter how much he was attacked, the hermit could not give an answer. Reflected in his bloodshot eyes were flames that even seemed to scorch the sky as they shot up from the village. The fire the spirit had brought with him from the village suddenly grew and ignited the hut, as well as the sandalwood and other trees in the garden. The hermit who resembled the spirit was enveloped in flames too. His screams were joined with those from the village.

The toad watched the flames as if puzzled, and, finally, with a gloomy croak, left the old pond and calmly went away. (*MHZ*, III, 106)

Japanese critics like to point to the obvious affinity between

Hakuchō's "Meimō" (Illusion) and the story "Mōsō" (Delusion) by Mori Ōgai, which also contains an old recluse contemplating time and existence.[11] However, Hakuchō himself felt that Ōgai was a man who was satisfied with objective reality, with just what he saw before him. Ōgai would fear death only when it was before him. Hakuchō claimed to have envied Ōgai his world view, one that was much less distressing than Hakuchō's deep concern for what might lie behind and beyond the surface of human reality.[12]

Hakuchō's "Illusion" and Ōgai's "Delusion" differ considerably. "Illusion" is a fantasy, whereas the Ōgai story is more of an apology for Ōgai's life. Much of the fantasy that characterizes "Illusion" seems borrowed from The Divine Comedy or Greek mythology, but "Delusion" contains no supernatural or fantastic elements. On the whole, it is a summation of Ōgai's intellectual and spiritual development, an outline of his reading, more or less, from the time of his study in Germany (1884–1888). It is prefaced and followed, however, by a sketch of an old man, who is more of a retired gentleman scholar than a passionate seeker of the meaning of life like the hero of "Illusion."

The old man in the Ōgai story seems but a metaphor for the philosophical detachment that Ōgai, whose personal reminiscences constitute most of the story, has achieved after decades of thought and study. Ōgai notes that the old man (Ōgai himself) spends his days "With the feeling of an unfinished dream, without fearing death, without longing for death."[13] Their respective philosophies aside, the image of the hermit in the Ōgai and the Hakuchō stories is one of a retired scholar in the Confucian mold in the former and one of a Taoist recluse, to some extent reminiscent of Han Shan and Shih-te, in the latter.

Both stories are tightly structured, for the most part, although Ōgai's "Delusion" does seem to bog down somewhat toward the end, as he apologizes for his many controversies, social as well as artistic or philosophical. Ultimately, the resemblance between the two stories seems to be something to be mentioned only briefly, for fear that dwelling on Hakuchō's debt to Ōgai might distract from an appreciation of "Illusion," which differs basically from "Delusion."

Still Hakuchō's reference to the obscure Mainlaender seems to imply that he was very conscious of the Ōgai story, in which Ōgai describes in some detail his initial exposure to Mainlaender's philosophy. Using a title similar to that of the Ōgai story, Hakuchō is, perhaps, telling his readers that his story will be a statement of his philosophy of life, in the same way "Delusion" expressed that of Ōgai.

The three apparitions in "Illusion" may be seen as creations of the old man's mind. They allow him (Hakuchō) to conduct a metaphysical dialogue with himself. The man answers the first apparition in Buddhist terms, telling that spirit that not only is a sixth sense not desirable, but the senses are the source of human suffering. The man answers the second apparition in Christian terms, telling that spirit that since life after death is inescapable one can only trust in the mercy of God.

It is significant in understanding Hakuchō's attitude toward Christianity at this time (1922) that, in reply, this second spirit points out the futility of expecting mercy from God. This echoes the psychology of Akiura, the psychotic hero of "Hell," whose paranoia is linked with his fear of the merciless, avenging Christian God.

The limitations of Buddhism and the contradictions of Christianity mean that they can offer the old man no consolation so that he is left confronting his self, the third spirit who resembles the hermit. Whereas Ōgai's hero can live on in quiet solitude with his "books ... a small Loupe ... a Zeiss microscope ... and, a Merz telescope,"[14] Hakuchō's more intense hero knows neither peace on earth nor life after death and must perish, both body (the old man himself) and soul (or "self," the third apparition).

The hermit's encounters with the three spirits reveal symbolically the philosophical dilemma that Hakuchō faced most of his life. That is, Hakuchō perceived only two equally unacceptable alternatives: pursuit of the irrational, religious faith, or acceptance of the terrible, the concept of total extinction at death. The third apparition (the hermit's soul) forces the old man to face the prospect of such total extinction. The first two spirits have shown that the peace to be gained through either Buddhist enlightenment or Christian immortality is illusory or insufficient.

The old man sees fundamental contradictions in both religions that preclude his accepting them. Buddhism strives for heightened awareness, but, to Hakuchō, this is a natural, rather than a supernatural, state. If Buddhism also teaches that our desires are the source of our suffering and that these desires arise from a need to gratify our senses, what can be gained from a heightening of our senses — in Hakuchō's words, an additional sense — but increased suffering?

There seems to be little hope of communication between the hermit and this first Buddhist spirit. The hermit dismisses him confidently and the spirit gives up on the man in disgust. It is the second, Christian spirit whose message upsets the man, for this spirit points out the contradictions of Christianity.

The basic contradiction is simple: how can man expect mercy from God, when He has created some people with natures that will guide them to eternal happiness and many others in such a way that their lives will lead inevitably to eternal damnation? Thus, the notion of the eternal soul brings horror as well as solace. The hermit is upset by the message of the apparition; he retreats to *The Divine Comedy* of Dante, the agent of the Christian God in his eyes.

It is significant that the hermit turns to *The Divine Comedy* to see the contradictions of Christianity — the contrast between the "frightening dreams" and the "beautiful dreams" — and not to a work of Christian theology, or even to the Bible itself. This shows that by the 1920s, if not earlier, Hakuchō turned to art, specifically literature, that expressed Christian sentiments, to judge the suitability of the religion as a personal faith for himself.

Through the first four decades or so of this century Hakuchō the writer, the man of letters, overshadowed Hakuchō the believer or skeptic, that is, Hakuchō the man. We always sense that for Hakuchō, at this time, Christianity was Dante, Strindberg, or Tolstoy, and not Christ or His apostles. Hakuchō's period of deepest introspection, as an evacuee during the last months of World War II, began a reversal of this relationship between his art and his philosophy, so that by the 1950s he had nearly lost hope in the ability of literature to express philosophical problems adequately. In this sense, throughout most of his life his literature stood in the way of his religion.

Uchimura Kanzō managed to combine an intense interest in literature with an apparently solid faith, but he always stressed the importance of the Gospels. It must be emphasized that Hakuchō, who had parted with Uchimura at about the turn of the century,[15] has his hermit reading Dante and not Matthew 5.

When the hermit's intimacy with *The Divine Comedy* and the immediacy of its language and imagery to him have been briefly established, the hermit is not given time for a conclusion about Christianity before the third and final spirit appears. This hints at Hakuchō's indecision concerning Christianity throughout most of his life. On the one hand, he is attracted to its notion of blind faith and, above all, to the complexity and genius of the literature it has inspired. On the other hand, however, he is repelled by the apparent absurdity and illogicality of Christianity's beliefs and contradictions.

What is left to him then is the conviction that there is no reason to expect an afterlife, that when man dies, his soul — assuming he has one — dies, too. The third apparition tells the hermit he is merely a man like any other; the hermit can expect no superhuman powers or supernatural states. In this view, certainly a modern one, man is left only with himself. He must confront himself and his world directly, blankly.

Hakuchō was not a scientist like Ōgai; he was unused to observing and classifying life calmly and coldly. The answer the third spirit brings is, thus, not a solution to Hakuchō, for it offers no peace. The prospect of total extinction, soul as well as body, is terrifying to him, and he expresses his terror through the agony — the flames and screams — of the reluctant hermit. No matter how much he is attacked and coerced, the hermit cannot say that he desires the nothingness of his own total extinction. The toad, who opens the story as a symbol of ugly, merely reproductive and thus purposeless, life, crawls away to continue the species in dark, meaningless gloom.

It is clear that even though Hakuchō finds little hope for peace in Buddhism and is unable to accept Christianity, although it intrigues him, he is, likewise, unwilling to adopt a mechanistic view of life. Such a view is, perhaps, all that remains to him once he has eliminated religion, but it is still a view that is alien to his nature. His fear of death and his persistent "religious sense" — his persistent "illusion" (*meimō*), as he termed it in 1957[16] — always called out for something beyond empirical explanations of life.

VI   *"I Killed a Man, And Yet" (1925) and the*
Thematic Structure of Hakuchō's Stories

Hakuchō was forty-six when "I Killed a Man, And Yet" was serialized in *Shūkan Asahi* from June to September, 1925. Twenty-one years had passed since the publication of his first story, "Solitude," in 1904; eighteen years since he first attracted attention with "Dust."

Twenty stories of the years 1904 to 1922 have been discussed; all clearly bear the stamp of Hakuchō's imagination; that is, the stories are unified thematically by Hakuchō's unrelenting philosophical concerns — the philosophical "heart" of Hakuchō's literature described in the discussion of "Nightmare" and "Various People."

This thematic unity is accompanied by structural similarity. The stories, whether autobiography or fantasy, contain a three-part exposition of the psychology of their characters. In nearly every story one or more characters are found in a state of psychological tension or isolation. The characters themselves, however, are aware only of effects, not their causes. Stories such as "Old Friend," "Peace of Mind," and "Suffocation" reverse the pattern and, in part at least, describe a character's fall from a state of bliss, but generally Hakuchō's characters are dissatisfied from the first.

Hakuchō's discontented characters are ignorant of the true dimensions of their dissatisfaction. Then, at some point, the second stage of their development occurs, in the form of a revelation. This "revelation" is often a brief incident, such as Kikuyo's "moment of clarity" in "The Smell of the Cowshed," which suddenly illuminates the full contour, the true shape of their unhappy lives. This sudden glare frequently casts a dark, disquieting shadow, and constitutes a moment of self-knowledge which usually leads not to peace of mind and understanding, but to a grimmer resolution.

Hakuchō's characteristically dark resolutions form the third structural segment of his stories. The progression is from twilight to bright light to darkness. The fact that Hakuchō's characters run instinctively from the light of revelation to the psychological shelter of dark corners justifies discussion of Hakuchō's literature in terms of its nihilism.

Hakuchō places his characters in a twilight area wherein both flight and confrontation with reality are possible. He then creates an incident that shows them the true face of both reality and themselves. A few characters are exceptional, but for the most part they shrink from this unforeseen truth.

The initial state of tension or isolation, broadly speaking, always involves aspects of desire. In fact, their unhappiness is always directly attributable to the presence or even absence of desire. When present, these desires are for success (especially artistic), for a woman, or, although rarely, for material gain.

Desire for artistic achievement is the most beguiling. In "Solitude" initially this desire both sustains and consumes Sawatani in his isolation. In "Old Friend" Inamura's desires for artistic success and the beautiful O-Sen are at first innocent and satisfying.

Obsession with a woman is a more dysphoric state, as is seen in Kiyoshi's love for O-Suma in "Discord and Harmony," the young narrator's infatuation with both O-Tane and O-Tama in "Suffocation," Sukejirō's yearning for his sister-in-law O-Sugi in "Until He Takes the Sleeping Medicine," and Toyomura's fascination with Tomoe in "Nightmare." On the other hand, for the comfortable Hakuchō, material desire was perhaps only a minor theme, but it does appear in "The Smell of the Cowshed." The material desire of Kikuyo and the old grandmother is reasonable but it renders them pathetic, rather than splendid, figures in the midst of their total poverty.

The negative aspects of a lack of desire are displayed in two ways: pathological or near-pathological isolation and vague but enervating feelings of emptiness and purposelessness. As for the former, the childhood gloom of Moriichi in "Ghost Picture" is established; likewise, young Akiura of "Hell" and the dreamer Sōkichi in "Wasted Effort" are, from the first, seen moving clearly toward a state of psychotic isolation. In "By the Inlet," the English teacher Tatsuo is perhaps not insane, but his eccentricity reaches dangerous extremes and he feels misunderstood and unhappy.

The most common type of discontented Hakuchō hero is the sane man struggling against despair in a world apparently devoid of meaning. This category includes the young man spying on his neighbors and reading the romances of Scott to escape bleak reality in "The Second-story Window," the young proofreader slipping into monotonous routine in "Dust," the restless, blasé Kenji in "Whither?", the cynical bridegroom Jūkichi in "Clay Doll," the dying husband in his initial confusion in "The Dead and the Living," the timorous, aimless Takayama in "Various People," and the doubting, tormented hermit in "Illusion."

As for the second phase of the thematic structure of Hakuchō's Meiji and Taishō stories, its revelations fall into three categories: unexpected dissatisfaction upon fulfillment of desires; a loss of interest in reality; and, most commonly, a shattering of illusions when the basis of hope proves unreal.

In the first category are the immediate loneliness of Sawatani when he achieves sudden artistic fame in "Solitude," Kenji's dejection at the loss of O-Tsuru to Minoura in "Whither?", and Jūkichi's restless frustration after his impulsive marriage in "Clay

Doll." Examples of the second category are the removal of the couple across the street from the student in "The Second-story Window," the touch of the woman which occasions Moriichi's crisis in "Ghost Picture," and the hallucinations and paranoia that provide Sōkichi in "Wasted Effort" with a new perception, allowing him to see imaginary snakes and fear an imagined tormentor.

Examples of the third category of "revelations," the shattering of illusions, are numerous. Kiyoshi's love for O-Suma is destroyed when he hears of her past in "Discord and Harmony." "Dust" is neatly divided into three segments; both its time and setting conform to and augment this structure. The first part, in which the narrator's general uneasiness is shown, is set during working hours at the newspaper office. The narrator's "revelation" occurs in a restaurant after work, when he learns that the lifeless Ono, too, had once had youthful hopes of escape from the dingy routine of the proofreader. The third segment, the resolution, occurs the next day back at the office. The focus of "Dust" is clearly on the process of exposing the true face of life to the young man. This is the destruction of man's "dreams," the *yume* to which Hakuchō often referred. Dreams and illusions must be cast aside to reveal the truth. Therefore, the scene in the restaurant occupies most of the story.

In the earlier "Old Friend," both the narrator Seiichi and his old friend, the Nara painter Inamura, have the veil of illusion drawn from their eyes by the same discovery, that of the worldliness of O-Sen. Although the events of "Old Friend" seem innocent, it is this knowledge about O-Sen that sets in motion forces that drive Seiichi from Christianity and Inamura into hiding among the Buddhist relics of Nara. Both feel man's hopelessly sinful nature has been revealed to them.

The delirious talk of Reverend Shibatani in "Peace of Mind" removes the narrator's illusions about man's true nature; insinuations about the virtue of the female caretaker in "Hell" remove Akiura's last source of communication, which leads to his total insanity. In the final scene of "Faint Light," O-Kuni's patron, Asakawa, shows that, after all, he does not love her any more than her previous men did, when he lightheartedly turns aside her talk of love suicide. In "Suffocation," the narrator's brash self-confidence and daydreams of a lucrative match with the voluptuous O-Tane are destroyed in an instant when he realizes how powerless he is to resist the advances of the slatternly O-Tama.

In "By the Inlet," the conversation between Eiichi and Tatsuo on the hill overlooking the bay reveals to them both the impossibility of communication; Tatsuo is also given a sense of his own insignificance and absurdity. Similarly, in "Until He Takes the Sleeping Medicine," O-Sugi's ridicule makes Sukejirō aware of his absurdity and isolation, and Kikuyo's "moment of clarity" allows her to admit the truth of what she overhears about herself while hiding in the boat in "The Smell of the Cowshed."

The "Nightmare" of Toyomura results from his sudden sense of the impossibility of fashioning a new life of happiness since his wife's control over his affairs is almost supernatural. Takayama's uneasiness in "Various People" comes from his knowledge that he is incapable of finding peace of mind through the only two means he knows: religion (Christianity) or a cathartic, physical act (murder). The inadequacy of Buddhism, Christianity, and Existentialism is revealed to the hermit of "Illusion" in spectacular, fiery fashion. In "The Dead and the Living," only the dying shopkeeper is allowed a transcendent, affirmative experience after the illusory nature of human affairs and desires is shown him by his illness.

Resolution, the third and final phase of the thematic structure of Hakuchō's Meiji and Taishō stories, takes the form of either a physical act or a psychological state. Physical resolution is achieved through suicide, murder, or flight.

Hakuchō's characters often think of suicide, but seldom act upon their suicidal impulses. Of these twenty stories, only "Until He Takes the Sleeping Medicine" contains a suicide. In "Ghost Picture," Moriichi plans to kill himself after murdering the idiot girl, but is spared suicide when she accidentally shoots him. Also, in "Sleeping Medicine," Hakuchō employs an ambiguous ending, a favorite device, to make Sukejirō's death seem likely but not absolutely certain.

Hakuchō's repressed characters are more likely to explode outwardly than to direct their impotent rage inward in an act of self-destruction. Besides Moriichi's attempted murder of the idiot girl, there are Toyomura's murder of his wife in "Nightmare," the enigmatic conclusion of "Illusion," and the murders in "I Killed a Man, And Yet," which we will describe.

A third form of physical resolution is flight. Although less dramatic than suicide or murder, Hakuchō frequently employs flight as resolution. Sawatani, in Hakuchō's first story "Solitude," flees the disillusionment of the hollow rewards of "success" by sailing to America. In "Old Friend," Inamura prefers to remain in seclusion in Nara rather than return to Tokyo and do battle with the artistic world. In "Whither?", Kenji wanders off to the safety of the anonymous streets of Tokyo. In "The Smell of the Cowshed," Kikuyo makes a bungled attempt at theft to finance her voyage away from the shame of her new self-knowledge; in "Various People," Takayama continues his restless migrations with his wife in tow.

Resolution occurs on a nonphysical level in two forms: insanity or, more commonly, ambiguous feelings and dim hopes. When Kiyoshi's image of O-Suma's purity shatters, he meekly succumbs to the quiet desperation of middle-class routine in "Discord and Harmony." In "The Second-story Window," the student takes solace in the remote romance of Scott, and in "Dust" the narrator has few illusions remaining as he halfheartedly puts faith in his youth.

The philosophical dilemma of the young Christian in "Peace of Mind" is resolved ironically, for he consoles himself for the loss of hope of salvation with the thought that at least he will not be going to Hell alone. The very title "Faint Light" evokes Hakuchō's notion of "trusting" in vague hopes for the future as the only course possible in the face of total uncertainties. Tokiko can turn to Buddhism for solace, but Jūkichi is left with only dissipation as "Clay Doll" ends on an indefinite note. As the events of "Suffocation" are resolved, the lucrative match with O-Tane seems a lost possibility, and the young suitor faces an uncertain fate at the hands of O-Tama, another man's mistress. The hopes for the future of the silent, misunderstood English teacher Tatsuo in "By the Inlet" are even dimmer.

In summary, Hakuchō's stories move from an opening state of tension or isolation to a second stage of illumination or revelation to the third and final stage, resolution. The initial dilemma is caused by desire (artistic, lustful, or material) or even by the absence of desire, the latter state characterized either by pathological (or almost pathological) isolation or feelings of emptiness and purposelessness. The illuminations and revelations of the second stage involve dissatisfaction with desires achieved, exposure of illusions, or a loss of touch with reality which leads to a new reality. Resolution, the third and final stage, is physical (suicide, murder, or flight) or nonphysical madness or a fading away into dim hopes and ambiguity.

The thematic structure of these twenty stories also characterizes perhaps Hakuchō's longest completed work of serious fiction, "I Killed a Man, And Yet." For example, the initial isolation of its protagonist, Tamotsu, is a result of his lack of desire, the empty, purposeless state in which he is first found.

Tamotsu is thirty-three, divorced, an unemployed teacher living in unrelieved boredom and idleness with his mother and younger brother. Tamotsu is attracted to a wealthy married woman, Tokiko. When her husband dies, presumably her victim, Tamotsu visits her. Entering quietly through the garden, Tamotsu overhears the dead man's brother arguing with Tokiko and accusing her of dealings with yet another man. When this brother happens to discover Tamotsu eavesdropping in the garden, there is a confrontation and Tamotsu strangles the brother with his bare hands.

The "other man" in the woman's life is charged with the crime but since he has a good alibi, the crime goes unsolved. The woman had been unaware of the scene in the garden, but in time she figures out who the murderer is. She is grateful to Tamotsu for ridding her of the problem of her husband's death; she pledges her love to Tamotsu.

"I Killed a Man," like "Nightmare," is about the thin line between dream and reality. Hakuchō made frequent use of this theme in his plays. There is a deliberate confusion in Tamotsu's perception of events meant to create a similar uncertainty in the mind of the reader, even though the story is told from the third-person point of view. The murder in the garden is completely unpremeditated; the frail Tamotsu finds it incredible that he was capable of such a brutal act of force. The irony of "I Killed a Man, And Yet" is that this sudden, spontaneous murder constitutes Tamotsu's revelation of his true character.

The role of murderer differs so much from both his self-image and the image others have of him that he begins to doubt the murder ever occurred. Bowing to the internal pressure created by this contradiction, in front of others he confesses his crime to a naive young girl he has happened to meet. Everyone treats his confession as a joke, and they refuse to believe him.

To prove to himself and to the world that the potent self revealed that night in the garden is true, he murders an old family friend. There are no witnesses. Tamotsu confesses his responsibility for this second murder to another friend who just laughs in disbelief. In the face of this further rejection Tamotsu tries to kill this young friend to prove to them both that he is really a murderer, but the younger man shoves him aside easily and still does not believe him.

The news reports of the old friend's death are brief and give cerebral hemorrhage as the cause. Tamotsu has failed to resolve his doubts about the truth of the first murder; he cannot get confirmation from the world that he is truly a murderer, that is, that he is potent and strong, not an impotent weakling. The first murder constitutes the second stage of the thematic structure, but the second murder is not a resolution but merely further partial revelation. It is then doubly ironic that even murder, which was previously a final, physical act resolving all psychological ambiguity, is no longer definite. Hakuchō's breach with reliance upon purely physical reality in his fiction has so widened that even death is no longer final.

As the story ends, Tamotsu is listening to his mother complain of how tired and worn she has become worrying about Tamotsu's recent eccentric behavior. He has confessed to her that he is a murderer, but ultimately she does not seem to appreciate that fact. Tamotsu feels great pity for his tired mother and, gazing at her, remarks that their recently deceased friend is resting in Paradise. All the while Tamotsu is thinking that he would like to send his mother to her final resting place, too. She sees the unpleasant gleam in her son's eyes and is struck by a dark foreboding.

Whereas the thematic structure of our previous twenty stories is 1-2-3, "I Killed a Man" has a different structure: 1-2a-2b-2n. Tamotsu kills a man, and yet no one, including himself, believes it. Therefore, he kills another man, and yet no one believes that, either. Finally, he seems on the point of killing another person, his mother[17] (the genderless *hito,* or "person," is used in the Japanese title), and perhaps, if there are no witnesses, no one will believe him again. The point is that there is no way of confirming truth ultimately, that only if nonexistence — the "extinction of the soul" in "Illusion" — follows death (here Tamotsu's) will there be finality. This will, presumably, provide true resolution.

CHAPTER 5

Dante

I *"On Dante" (1927)*

The Bible is an absorbing book. Although I neither believe in the Christian God nor submit to the doctrines of Christianity, even I regard it (Old and New Testaments in one volume) as one of my favorite books, one which I must keep at hand throughout my life. Because I enjoy reading the Bible as ancient history, as a record of humanity, as sincere poetry and as artless fiction, I do not summon much interest for such righteously indignant books of prophecy as Isaiah and Jeremiah, or for the evangelistic Epistles of Paul. I find the life of modern man reflected clearly in the stories of ancient man in Genesis, such as in stories of how Eve tempted Adam, Cain slew his brother out of jealousy, Esau sold his birthright to his brother for pottage, and Joseph was falsely accused by his master's wife because he rejected her advances. I feel such books as Exodus and Leviticus are like realistic novels depicting the collective life of man. (*MHZ,* VII, 93)

IT is clear from this opening paragraph of Hakuchō's key essay "On Dante" that he did not consider himself a Christian in 1927. Equally clear, however, is the strength of Hakuchō's continued attachment to the literature of this religion he rejected.

Hakuchō relates that his first exposure to Dante was through an essay by Lord Macaulay on Milton. Hakuchō next encountered Dante in Carlyle's "On Heroes, Hero-Worship and the Heroic in History," to which he was led by Uchimura's lectures in the 1890s. Hakuchō proudly states that he purchased his own copy of Henry Francis Cary's English translation of *The Divine Comedy* on June 19, 1905, and that he still frequently takes that well-worn volume with him on his travels, "to recite a canto or a verse here and there, whenever I please" (*MHZ,* VII, 94).

Hakuchō finds the language of "Heroes and Hero-Worship"

"majestic and intense." In particular, he admires Carlyle's statement that "in Dante had ten silent centuries finally found a voice."
Hakuchō goes on to say.

> Today, several decades after first hearing it, I am reminded of that typi-
> cally Carlylean epithet, "Dante's *Divine Comedy,* the medieval voice of
> ten silent centuries," whenever I read the *Divine Comedy.* It seems a con-
> tradiction, but from some twenty years ago, when I believed in Christian-
> ity, until today, when I dislike Christianity and its believers, I have been
> drawn to the Middle Ages of Europe. It is only natural that I have long
> knelt in reverence before the *Divine Comedy,* which embodies the human-
> ity of the Middle Ages. (*MHZ,* VII, 95)

Hakuchō quotes *The Divine Comedy* frequently and at length.
His quotes include: the opening tercet; the dark inscription atop the
gates of Hell (Inferno, III, 1–9); the long conversation between
Dante and the painter Oderigi, who is being cleansed of the sin of
pride (Purgatory, XI, 79–102); the words of Guido del Duca
(Purgatory, XIV, 82–4); the famous lament of Francesca: " 'No
greater grief than to remember days / Of joy, when misery is at
hand...' "[1] (Inferno, V, 121–2); the confession of the envious
Lady Sapia that she was " 'gladder far / Of other's hurt, than of
the good befel me,' "[2] (Purgatory, XIII, 110–111); and, Dante's
resolve to steel himself for his journey into Hell (Inferno, II, 3–5).
  Hakuchō alludes to many other passages; he even finds time for
a summary of the state of Dante scholarship in Japan in 1927. He
also refers frequently to Western opinions of Dante, rejecting the
attacks of Goethe upon Dante and preferring the praise of J.A.
Symonds in his *Introduction to the Study of Dante* and C.H.
Grandgent in *The Power of Dante.* Like Symonds, Hakuchō
prefers Matilda of the Terrestrial Paradise to Dante's idealized Beatrice; like Grandgent he longs for the unhurried approach to literature characteristic of the Middle Ages but nearly impossible amid
the flood of inconsequential modern publications.
  Hakuchō is attracted to the theme of exile which he sees as domi-
nating both the life of Dante and the figures of Virgil and Dante in
The Divine Comedy. Hakuchō quotes Paradise, XVII, 55–60,
which is a prophecy of future unhappiness in Dante's own life by
Dante's ancestor, Cacciaguida, who warns Dante "shalt prove /
How salt the savour is of other's bread."[3]
  Hakuchō is especially drawn to the description of a monastery at
the foot of a mountain, which is being related to Dante by someone

else in Paradise, XXI, but which Hakuchō feels refers to the actual monastery where Dante took refuge while in political exile. Hakuchō even feels compelled to provide his own underlining:

> ...There
> So firmly to God's service I adhered,
> *That with no costlier viands than the juice*
> *Of olives, easily I pass'd the heats*
> *Of summer and the winter frosts;* content
> In heaven-ward musing....[4]

This is perhaps Dante's own experience, but he was unable to remain in that sacred place, simply adoring God and contemplating eternity, or lost in poetic composition. He soon re-emerged, received the patronage of various members of the nobility, and tasted "how salt the savour is of other's bread." Dante willingly put himself in a position where he might call forth both scorn and respect. The murmur of the monk standing in the darkness of a monastery — "Oh, blessed solitude! Oh, sole blessing!" — still echoes in my ears, six hundred years later, and, in spite of myself, I must hang my head. (*MHZ*, VII, 103)

Hakuchō stands in admiration of the power of Dante's poetry to communicate truth, which is for Hakuchō that which is true to life. However, as we have seen from the opening paragraph of "On Dante," Hakuchō remains an admirer, not a believer. In this connection, Hakuchō expresses doubts about the ability of literature to communicate faith; he was still expressing these doubts during the last year of his life, as we have also seen.

As has been universally noted, the apparent point of the *Divine Comedy* is that man can be saved by love, symbolized by Beatrice, but not by reason, symbolized by Virgil. But the descriptions of Paradise are exceedingly dry and insipid to us. With the gulf between our age and Dante's that is unavoidable, but what might be the reason that I, among others, cannot feel the light of Beatrice's love keenly? Life's sublime state of ecstasy, the attainment of love or salvation, is perhaps difficult to convey with words. The phenomena of suffering and sorrow, recited in poetry, expressed in writing, can be communicated to others, but a state of contentment, perhaps, cannot be expressed with words. (*MHZ*, VII, 104)

What is disappointing, however, is that in discussing this inability of Beatrice and the Paradise to move us in the way Matilda and both the Inferno and Purgatory do, Hakuchō does not pursue a metaphysical explanation. Rather, Hakuchō, characteristically, prefers to keep his feet firmly on the ground and seek a biographical explanation for the "failure" of Beatrice as a character. He cites Boccaccio's alleged description of Dante's wife Gemma as an oppressively suspicious woman to show that it was natural that Dante was consoled by memories of the young girl Beatrice. The failure of Beatrice is that of a fantasy girl, who must lack vitality since she had no flesh and blood model. Hakuchō even mentions the wives of Milton, Strindberg, and Tolstoy, which must have delighted Kobayashi Hideo. Fortunately, Hakuchō specifically disdains applying a Freudian interpretation of the Paradise as "a manifestation of Dante's repressed sexual desire for Beatrice" (*MHZ*, VII, 104), because that would ultimately do damage to the "divinity" of Dante's work.

In the end, it is the spirituality of the Middle Ages that gives *The Divine Comedy* more meaning to Hakuchō than any other work of literature, Japanese, Western, or otherwise.

. . . I have no interest in theology, but I envy the state of mind of the people of the Middle Ages. I even aspire to it. Therein, undoubtedly, was manifest a tranquil state of ecstasy, utterly denied modern civilized man. "The soul" was "A pilgrim on earth"; "This world is a night's temporary lodging; home was on the other side" — abandon everything and go to a monastery! There, "with no costly viands than the juice / Of olives, easily I pass'd the heats / Of summer and the winter frosts."

According to superficial historical accounts, the Middle Ages were the so-called Dark Ages, when the common people lived lives of misery under the despotic government of priests and monarchs. However, their dark despotic world may be considered different from the gloomy peace under the government of the Tokugawa. Rather than lowly people squirming aimlessly beneath oppression, they may be thought of as having dreamed beautiful dreams during their ephemeral lives. Since their complicated philosophy, also, was of service as a potion to bring on these dreams, it was not without use to them. I reflect, " 'Is it not, after all, a night's temporary lodging?' Be the world round or be it flat, let it revolve or not, such things may be as they will — they were not frightened by thoughts of uncertainty, as they waited for their earthly pilgrimage to end." Is it not perhaps enough if man can attain that much? (*MHZ*, VII, 105)

II   *Hakuchō and* The Divine Comedy

Hakuchō's interest in *The Divine Comedy* is personal, not scholarly. When he feels human existence is marked by suffering, he turns to Dante for relief from the pain of existence. Hakuchō has little interest in purely theological questions, such as peculiarly Christian concepts of sin. To begin the third of the three sections of "On Dante," Hakuchō relates an anecdote about the life of Dante that has special meaning for Hakuchō himself:

Legend has it that, during his wanderings, Dante even went to Paris. On the way, when he asked for lodging at a certain monastery, a monk there asked him as he did of all travellers, "What do you seek coming here?" The monk was surprised that Dante did not answer, so he asked the same question again. Whereupon, Dante is said to have replied in a single word, "Peace."

Because of this anecdote, I have long admired Dante's state of mind. (*MHZ,* VII, 102–103)

Like Dante on his journey to Paris, Hakuchō seeks peace. Hakuchō desires a refuge from the pain he feels in life, but he also has a strong fear of death.

Since death awaits every man, exclusive preoccupation with this life is, in the end, unavailing, whether or not there is an afterlife. Hakuchō's quotations of his favorite passages from *The Divine Comedy* underscore the fact that he held this conviction. The futility of pride, ambition, and worldly fame is obviously the point, for Dante and Hakuchō, of the example of such figures as the painter Oderigi. But each man must live out his life, whether because, as a Christian, he disdains the sin of despair or because, like Hakuchō, he fears death.

Hakuchō looks for models among the literary figures of the West; he seeks an example to follow in finding peace and an accommodation of his fear of death. In "On Dante," Hakuchō at one point compares *The Divine Comedy* with Strindberg's "To Damascus." He finds the difference between the two men more superficial than might be supposed, simply the difference between medieval and modern methods of expression. He sees Strindberg going through the same spiritual exercise that Dante describes in *The Divine Comedy.*

And, Strindberg, that modern poet of Northern Europe, also, passed through a seemingly modern form of hell and purgatory. There he tempered his soul, before at last seeking peace in his old age in a state of religious rapture in Catholicism. (*MHZ,* VII, 98)

Hakuchō realizes that he, too, like Dante and Strindberg, must pass through his own spiritual hell or purgatory before attaining the salvation of his paradise. His salvation will be his peace, and it is clear that he knows that this peace must come through belief. The question throughout Hakuchō's life was what to believe in, not whether to believe. His doubts were of the existence of anything, be it in art or religion, that could compel such belief. Further, he doubted his strength, not will, to believe.

On the one hand, the exile of Dante is a metaphor to Hakuchō of the trials that mark the life of every man. On the other, however, Hakuchō is impressed with the fact of Dante's personal, real-life misfortunes. Hakuchō is puzzled, at first, that Dante's work is not more of an autobiography in a stricter sense, but is satisfied, in the end, with the historical explanations he has uncovered. Most significantly, however, there was no need for Dante to relate the facts of his own life in *The Divine Comedy* because his was a spiritual biography, and, after all, as Hakuchō saw it, for Dante, the voice of the Middle Ages, true reality was in the afterlife, in the world beyond.

Humility springs naturally from a belief in an afterlife, for such belief renders futile any excessive attachment to this life, that is, again, to pride, ambition, and fame. Hakuchō admires what he sees as Dante's "realism," but, of course, this refers to the believability, and thus the universality, of the suffering of the sinners depicted in Dante's Inferno and Purgatory. All of these accounts are products of Dante's imagination, but such punishments as those of the gluttons and usurers (Inferno: V; XVII) are so apt that they seem "real" to him. In "On Dante" Hakuchō also describes the topicality of *The Divine Comedy* for the Florentine reader of Dante's day. This adds to its believability, its "realism," in Hakuchō's eyes, and brings forth all the more admiration.

It is the fundamental humanity of Dante, as much as anything, that earns Hakuchō's sympathy and allows him to identify with Dante. Had Dante adopted a more thoroughly vindictive and superhumanly pious or "divine" tone (had he not immediately shown pity for his old teacher Brunetto (Inferno, XV) or not been prey to anger himself, for example) it is unlikely he would have gained such consistent attention and admiration from Hakuchō. Dante's supposed dissatisfaction with his wife and his subsequent fantasies of Beatrice are, also, readily understandable to Hakuchō's mind. To be sure, Hakuchō feels it fitting to characterize

Dante's writing as "divine," but it is ultimately the believability and universality that he finds in Dante's attitude toward women that impresses Hakuchō most.

The "beautiful dreams" of the people of the Middle Ages represent an escape from the unpleasant reality of both the "Dark Ages" and twentieth-century Japan. However, more than just as escape, they should be seen as attractive to Hakuchō because through such "dreams" medieval man focused on the essential philosophical problems of human existence. To some, it may seem an obvious, even hackneyed, complaint, but Hakuchō is discontented with the rapid pace and mundane banality of modern life.

Modern life has little spiritual content, and Hakuchō sees the Middle Ages as a time when man was freer than now from external distractions, and could reflect in solitude, like the medieval monk, upon purely spiritual matters of the soul. The meaningless strain and the ultimate futility of trying to keep up with the bewildering profusion of new publications is linked with what Hakuchō regards as the lamentable modern disregard of the nobility of books, as well as with Hakuchō's longing for the sense of awe and uninterrupted pleasure he associates with his reading as a youth.

To live in blissful solitude and to be free of the fear of death: these are Hakuchō's own dreams which he sees fulfilled in his idealization of medieval man. The question of whether or not Hakuchō found the ability to believe and thus overcame his fear of death is, of course, bound up with the discussion of his last years and death. He did turn to Christianity in the end, as we have seen, and the implications of his return and its significance to Japanese thought and literature generally, as well as simply to Hakuchō's own story, are of major proportions. Nevertheless, it is unclear from "On Dante" exactly what direction his thought would take.

Examination of the question of religious belief, or even expressions of longing for the ability to believe, do not make one a believer. Hakuchō must be taken at his word when he says in 1927 that he "neither believes in the Christian God nor submits to the doctrines of Christianity." There is little evidence that he "believed" in anything during this period — Christianity, Buddhism, or art.

The ideal of blissful solitude, symbolized by Hakuchō's image of the medieval "monk standing in the darkness of a monastery," was to remain in Hakuchō's thoughts, it seems, although it never led him to any drastic changes in his life. In 1948 he rented a small room on the sixth floor of an apartment house in Tokyo, which he used, until 1956, for his monthly and bimonthly visits from his home in Karuizawa. He would stay five or six days in Tokyo to submit his manuscripts and collect his remuneration from his publishers.[5]

Hakuchō had his adopted son live alone in Tokyo, and when in Tokyo Hakuchō would stay by himself in his "apartment." Having the three members of his small family in three different places was uneconomical and rather lonely, but he felt that only when he was alone could he reflect upon things of philosophical significance. For amusement Hakuchō enjoyed walking about among the crowds in Tokyo, present as an observer rather than a participant in life.[6]

Considering his means, age, and position, Hakuchō's Tokyo surroundings were Spartan, but his lifestyle was always unmaterialistic,[7] as we would expect of the author of "On Dante." Hakuchō was not notably talkative, although at dinner and when the conversation turned to literature he was at times surprisingly eloquent.[8]

For most of his life he was bothered by insomnia. Kobayashi Hideo, after visiting Hakuchō, described him as an "evacuee from life."[9] Hakuchō's indifference to clothing and to style, too, seems to have been a legend.[10] Like his medieval monk, he regarded this world as "a temporary dwelling." However, although he was admittedly lonely at times, the picture of the elderly Hakuchō walking about the crowded streets of Tokyo (all the while, perhaps, dreaming "of a corner of heaven") or reading at night in his small, bare rented room is, for the reader of "On Dante," not one of a lonely man, but merely one of a man alone.

Hakuchō finds much in *The Divine Comedy* and the life of Dante upon which to focus his critical attention: the futility of attachment to this life, certainly not an exclusively Christian thought, especially for a Japanese; the "realism" of *The Divine Comedy;* Dante's humanity; longing for peace; and the comfort of solitude. To this list may be added the notion of exile and estrangement, which is the dominant fact of Dante's life and is also central to *The Divine Comedy.* Not only is exile a theme which the critic of Dante would naturally treat, but it seems another ingredient in Dante and his work contributing to Hakuchō's special feelings for Dante.

"How salt the savour is of other's bread" — a sentiment from *The*

Divine Comedy that was an especial favorite of Hakuchō. However, even taking into account the moves that led him to Ōiso, there is little in Hakuchō's own life to suggest a basis for a physical identification with the sorrow of Dante's exile. Hakuchō knew little unusual hardship in his life, other than persistent childhood illness. He was never truly poor or disadvantaged in any way. In Tokyo, as a young man, his talent and intellectual potential soon established him as a budding member of the literary intelligentsia, as we have seen.

Explanations for Hakuchō's attraction to the theme of exile must be sought in the fact that he was always an introspective and deeply religious person from the time of his childhood frailty, religious searching, and copious reading, throughout the sixty some years of his career. His attraction to the notion of exile indicates a spiritual bond he felt with Dante as a spiritual exile.

We have seen the persistent feelings of personal estrangement from the life around one in Hakuchō's earliest fiction, an attitude that can certainly be described in terms of the now well-worn, but still quite serviceable term "alienation." In many instances it is easily and specifically identifiable, but often it is much more vaguely felt and obliquely perceived. In "On Dante" Hakuchō desires such estrangement, or rather seeks to change its character, to turn what appears a burdensome, sometimes oppressive, psychological isolation in his early fiction into the splendid solitude of his idealized medieval monk.

Hakuchō lightly rebukes his former mentor Uchimura Kanzō for presuming to identify too enthusiastically with the exiled Dante;[11] Hakuchō himself, he would have us believe, would not be so presumptuous. Still, the forlorn figure of Virgil, the symbol of reason, turned away from Paradise to remain forever in Limbo, had additional meaning for Hakuchō, who, in terms of his acceptance of Christianity, was in much the same position. Within the religious context of *The Divine Comedy,* Virgil, too, is an exile; to the Christian, whatever Virgil's gifts and attainments, his estrangement is devastating, for he is estranged from the sight of God. Hakuchō, at this time, believed in nothing, but it is clear from his "envy" of medieval man that he wanted to believe in something.

Hakuchō obviously felt a tremendous sense of loss, ruled, like Virgil, by his reason, which told him there was nothing to believe in, but never totally free of the feeling that somehow he would have to believe in something to find peace. Because of the hold of reason upon Hakuchō's beliefs, he found himself an exile from his own heart. To this uneven chain of exiles — Dante, Virgil, Uchimura — is added one more disparate link: Hakuchō, "evacuee from life."

III   *The West, Literary Criticism, and "On Dante"*

"On Dante" says much about Hakuchō's relation to the West and Western literature, his critical attitude, and the nature of his literary criticism. Hakuchō had long and varied dealings with the West: as a youth attending missionary services in Okayama; a convert to Christianity during his early days in Tokyo; an increasingly sophisticated student of the Western literary tradition; a wide-eyed tourist seeing firsthand the pervasiveness of white discrimination against Orientals in Europe and especially America in 1928–1929; and, finally, as an evacuee in Karuizawa, escaping the World War II bombings, to which he lost his Tokyo home in 1945.

Throughout this long acquaintanceship, which includes both positive and negative experiences, Hakuchō's West was one of ideas. There is little pettiness or bitterness in his attitude. The West, for Hakuchō, was Dante and Goethe, or Carlyle and Reverend Henry Francis Cary, not the condescending, indifferent Americans and Europeans at whose mercy Hakuchō frequently found himself, while travelling with his wife.

To some extent, Hakuchō conceived of literature in a Western, more than an Asian, context, so that he often appears to be outside of his own tradition. That statement can be made of many modern Japanese men of letters, but, even in Hakuchō's case, it is only true to a point. Hakuchō had no two-way interaction with Western literature — he was aware of it, but it was unaware of him — and, too, he was, and remains, a key figure in twentieth-century Japanese literary history, which he may have perceived in the 1920s, if not earlier.

Moreover, Hakuchō did respond to his own native literary tradition, although less often and not as fully as such "traditional" writers as Tanizaki, Mishima, and Kawabata. Hakuchō mentions his early love of *kabuki* in "On Dante." He also describes rapt reading in his "timeworn second-story room" in Honami, which included many *kusazōshi* (Edo period illustrated storybooks), Bakin's *Hakkenden* (The Lives of Eight Dogs), the works of Saikaku (whose realism he praised), and the *Heike Monogatari* (The Tale of the Heike), which Hakuchō admired for its poetic beauty.

Although not mentioned in "On Dante," Hakuchō's relationship to the most important product of the Japanese classical tradition, the *Genji Monogatari* (The Tale of Genji), is of great interest. Much can be learned of the makeup of Hakuchō's intellect from the simple fact that he was unable to respond to the *Genji Monogatari* until he decided — in 1933! — to read the famous English translation by Arthur Waley. He was full of praise for *Genji* after this experience, for he realized the breadth of world literature, that it was not just the fiction of great Western writers, such as Balzac and Dostoyevsky.

Hakuchō said that the experience was "like standing on the heights and gazing at the broad blue star-filled sky." He was most impressed with the "Kashiwagi" and the two "Wakana" (New Herbs) sections, as well as the final chapter, "The Bridge of Dreams."[12] Upon comparing the English version with the Japanese original, Hakuchō found that while the Waley translation was a work of genius, the original was also to be admired for its clean, terse style. Hakuchō appreciated the fictional style of *Genji,* but found it extremely difficult to read in the Heian original.[13]

Hakuchō's reaction to the Waley version of *Genji* and not to the original may be an indication that he understood modern English better than classical Japanese. But then again it may be some indication of feelings of cultural inferiority toward the West. It may be a facet of the cultural syndrome that fails to recognize the fact of native genius until it has proved itself by its acceptance abroad. At least two facts support speculation that a cultural inferiority complex of sorts entered into his opinions: his lifelong involvement with Christianity, and his buying the English version of *Genji* on the spur of the moment one day because he had heard what a reputation it was enjoying in the West.[14]

It is admirable that Hakuchō conceived of fiction in terms of a world literature, but regrettable that until 1933 he did not fully include his own literary tradition. However, his reaction could also be an indication of the sometimes alleged superiority of the Waley version over the Japanese original. Or, perhaps, Hakuchō's rereading of the classic in English just chanced to be the occasion for his finally appreciating *Genji* for the masterpiece it is.

In his long and productive career Hakuchō's criticism would range from Homer and Dante to contemporary Japanese writers. His criticism was sometimes resented, and this led to quarrels with such literary figures as Tokuda Shūsei, on more than one occasion,

and Nagai Kafū, who, when he was not replying in rebuttal to
Hakuchō's remarks about his own works, was criticizing Hakuchō's writing. Gotō Ryō feels that, considering the range of their
quarrels, the fact that Hakuchō insisted all of his life that he liked
Kafū shows considerable self-restraint on his part.[15]

Ōiwa Kō describes this aspect of Hakuchō's criticism by the
English term "negative capability." This term was "used by Keats
to describe the objective and impersonal aspects of Shakespeare
. . . and has since been applied to the qualities in an artist's work
which enable him to avoid in it the expression of his own personality."[16] Ōiwa feels it applies to Hakuchō's criticism more than to
that of any other Japanese critic.[17]

Such a trait is especially noteworthy in the light of the fact that
many Japanese critics are inclined toward a biographical approach
to literature, one that links aspects of a literary work with those of
the author's life or personality. Hakuchō himself often, although
not exclusively, used such a biographical approach — that is
evident even from "On Dante." Moreover, he freely interjects his
own personality and, frequently, autobiographical elements into
his literary criticism. Therefore, Gotō's comments on Hakuchō's
criticism are of even more interest.

The chief characteristics of Hakuchō's criticism are, in Gotō's
view, a strong "backbone" and deep insight, a keen cutting edge to
his critical opinions, and the inclusion of a wealth of literary
gossip. He sees this tendency toward gossip to be a natural result of
Hakuchō's newspaper days when as a critic he met almost all the
figures of the literary establishment and knew them well, thus
reducing the distance between himself and the authors he criticized.[18] Such an essay as "A Study of Natsume Sōseki" (*"Natsume
Sōseki-ron"*), which appeared in the *Chūō Kōron,* June, 1928,
exhibits all of these characteristics and provides a better example of
Hakuchō's tendency toward literary gossip than "On Dante" does.

While not totally denying Hakuchō's "negative capability," we
must conclude that, rather than an attitude of objectivity, what set
Hakuchō off from many other Japanese critics was his sense of the
vast possibilities of literature and of a higher critical standard for
literature derived from his familiarity with such Western masters as
Dante, Goethe, and Strindberg. Hakuchō's relative critical detachment, lofty standards, and natural seriousness combined to produce a critical attitude that recognizes only true art and bestows
praise begrudgingly. Herein would seem to lie a significant con-

tribution to early twentieth-century Japanese literary criticism.

"On Dante" is not marked by a detached critical attitude; it tells as much about Hakuchō as it does about Dante, if not more. The narrative may focus upon Dante or Dante scholarship for a while, but Hakuchō's attention always returns to what *The Divine Comedy* and the life of Dante mean to Hakuchō himself. This aspect may be particularly fascinating to the Japanese reader.

Japanese literary criticism often tends to be journalistic in character. Considering the "popular" nature of much Japanese criticism, however, "On Dante" shows great love for the subject, attention to detail, and considerable understanding of Dante. The Japanese reader of that day must have learned from "On Dante" much about Dante and *The Divine Comedy,* and equally about Hakuchō's philosophical outlook and artistic sensibility.

Another facet of his criticism that is revealed in "On Dante" is his persistent demand for "realism." An essay on a medieval poet hardly seems the place for the critic to speak of realism, but Hakuchō, at least through the 1920s, held a work's "realism" — by which he often meant its "believability," as we noted — to be the supreme test of its success.

In "A Study of Natsume Sōseki," for example, Hakuchō frequently disparages Sōseki for writing fiction that does not create "reality" (*sesō*). He asserts repeatedly that he would not deny that Sōseki was a great writer, but he finds him to be concerned with plot above all and to rely upon contrived situations and literary devices.

Hakuchō admires the realism of Sōseki's autobiographical *Michikusa* (Grass on the Wayside) (1915), as well as that of his unfinished *Meian* (Light and Darkness) (1916). In Hakuchō's view, *Meian's* realism compensates for its tediousness, for it is free of the attempts at lyricism and the romantic flourishes which, he feels, mar Sōseki's earlier works (*MHZ,* VI, 143–144).

Likewise, in "On Dante," there are many references to the "reality" of *The Divine Comedy.* Although Hakuchō clearly states that he no longer has any use for the archetypical Japanese "I" novel, long on veracity but short on inspiration, he still must discuss literature in terms of its "reality." Among the many similar terms Hakuchō employs in "On Dante" to refer to this problem are *"genjitsu"* (actuality), *"jijitsu"* (fact), and *"shajitsu no myō"* (realistic genius).

In the postwar period Hakuchō showed his dissatisfaction with the ability of literature to resolve existential and religious problems, following an increasing disenchantment with realistic fiction. However, even by the time of "On Dante," Hakuchō's conception of "realism" had been stretched beyond the usual limits of the term. Hakuchō described as "realistic" that literature which made the reader feel the universality of literary experience and how it relates to human experience. In time he despaired of finding literature that truly re-creates the spiritual depths of human experience, but he never abandoned literature, perhaps because of the example of such spiritual and literary ancestors as Dante and *The Divine Comedy.*

CHAPTER 6

Plays

OF his forty plays, Hakuchō wrote six in 1924, eight in 1925, five in 1926, and seven in 1927. There was considerable theatrical activity in Tokyo in the mid-1920s. The theatrical groups included the Bungei-za, Shingeki Kyōkai, Shunjū-za, Dainiji Geijutsu-za (from February, 1924), and the Tsukiji Shōgekijō (opened under the direction of Osanai Kaoru in June, 1924).[1]

Hakuchō rode this wave of activity by renewing his career as a dramatist. As we have seen, his first dramatic work was *White Wall* in 1912 and his second, *The Secret,* in 1914. He felt the content of his plays would probably be about the same as that of his fiction, being after all by the same man. Still, he was tired of *shōsetsu* and also enjoyed the challenge of writing with the aim of making characters come alive on the stage. Hakuchō claimed to be referring to the stage of his mind's eye, however, for he stated that he did not write his plays expecting them to be performed in a theater, and that if they were it would simply be a matter of luck.[2]

Be that as it may, most of Hakuchō's plays were performed soon after their composition. However, to take him at his word and accept this ruse, at least in part, Hakuchō wanted merely to borrow the form of the drama, with its almost total dependence upon dialogue, to achieve greater ambiguity.

The biographical fact of Hakuchō's early involvement with Christianity and the explicitly religious content of many of his earlier stories lead to an expectation of the appearance of religious elements in all of his works. Likewise, the frequently deliberate ambiguity of his use of supernatural elements leads to a similar expectation of intimations of the supernatural.

Hakuchō's plays, even more consistently than his fiction, try to maneuver the audience into a state wherein the unlikely, the supernatural, explanation seems almost possible. Not all of his plays follow this course; some are concerned mostly with an easily identifiable, "common sense" view of reality. However, the most effective plays — thematically, and, perhaps, also, dramatically — are almost invariably those that contain fantasy or psychological ambiguity.

I   Shadows *(1924)*

Shadows appeared in the *Chūō Kōron* in February, 1924, but it was not performed in the 1920s. It was finally done, however, in 1965, by the little semiprofessional theater group *Kaze*. This remarkable troupe of fewer than twenty members has determinedly attempted to stage at least one Hakuchō play annually as part of its offerings since 1963. Although Hakuchō is by no means a major playwright and many people are even unaware that he wrote plays, a small cult of admirers, fortunately, keeps his dramas alive.

Surprisingly, Hakuchō's plays do not resemble *kabuki* plays. Noda Yūji, an original member[3] and current director of *Kaze,* has been involved in perhaps a score of productions of Hakuchō's plays over the past fifteen years. He feels the roots of Hakuchō's plays are in Western drama, particularly the works of Ibsen, Chekhov, and Strindberg. For example, *The Joys of Life* (see Section II) Noda regards as influenced by the works of Ibsen and Strindberg.

Postwar productions of Hakuchō's plays, both by *Kaze* and other theatrical troupes, have employed a consistently modern acting style far removed from that of *kabuki*. As modern Japanese plays in the twentieth-century *shingeki* (new drama) tradition, Hakuchō's dramas are faster paced and, not surprisingly, much more concerned with realism than those of *kabuki*. However, Noda reasons, inasmuch as *kabuki* and *shimpa* (new school [of *kabuki*]) actors were frequently involved in the prewar productions of Hakuchō's plays, they may have exhibited considerable *kabuki* influence.

One of Hakuchō's major objectives in coming to Tokyo in the 1890s was to see *kabuki,* as we have noted. At that time, before the advent of *shingeki, kabuki* was perhaps the most modern theater form available. Thus, the great role of Western influence in Hakuchō's intellectual development and the fact that Hakuchō's plays are written in a "modern," or "Western," style, lead Noda to the conclusion that rather than always stress Hakuchō's fondness for *kabuki,* we should say that Hakuchō was fond of "theater."

Shadows takes place in the Western-style study of the writer Suhara Seitarō. He and his wife Yoshiko are discussing how to preserve the middle-class serenity of their lives, which calm is about to be assaulted by the imminent visit of a Mr. Toda, an old friend of Suhara. Toda has lived in relative seclusion in the country since a young interloper stole his wife Tomiko nearly twenty years before.

Suhara and Yoshiko are also fretting over their daughter Kuniko's unenthusiastic attitude toward the marriage they have arranged for her. They are afraid Kuniko may still be longing for an earlier suitor, Ōmura, of whom they totally disapprove. They view the visit of the hapless Toda at such a delicate juncture in Kuniko's life as an ill omen.

To their surprise, Toda and Kuniko arrive together. Toda has chanced upon her on the streetcar, introduced himself, and begun a frank, personal discussion with her. Kuniko is drawn out of her gloom and reserve immediately; her parents note right away her unaccustomed animation.

Toda contrasts with Suhara. Toda is associated with rural calm; Suhara with the noisy confusion of Tokyo. Toda is naive but immediately concerned with Kuniko's happiness; Suhara is a sophisticated writer but cruel to his daughter in the name of discharging his social obligations. Toda intuitively perceives Kuniko's unhappiness over her coming marriage, whereas Suhara is not perceptive at all. Toda reveals all, holding back nothing; he is even referred to as a "sage." Suhara, on the other hand, is hypocritical; he writes about such things as the "sanctity of truth," but, unlike Kuniko, is deaf to the truth of what Toda says about life and unhappiness.

Toda is a character of the heart and Suhara of the mind. In both Western and Japanese fiction, from the works of Nathaniel Hawthorne to those of Kawabata Yasunari, it is possible to identify "heart characters," naive, instinctive, honest characters like Toda, and "head characters," sophisticated, reserved, and deceptive like Suhara. But all the characters are aspects of one literary and intellectual entity: Hakuchō's imagination, or thought. In Hakuchō's literature this bipolar tension is manifest in the coexistence of his metonymic and metaphorical tendencies. That is, such bipolarity is expressed through his predilection not only for realistic fiction, but also for plays and the fantastic.

In his life, Hakuchō expressed this tension in terms of a philosophical choice between the logicality of atheism and the irrational-

ity of belief in Christianity. Awareness of this literary and philosophical bipolarity is crucial in understanding Hakuchō's writing
and thought. For, even if tomorrow some irrefutable piece of evidence were somehow unearthed disputing Hakuchō's deathbed
conversion, the fact of his lifelong literary and personal doubting
and struggle would remain unaffected by such revelations.

Toda, in *Shadows,* recalls Hakuchō's conception of Dante. Toda
states explicitly that his journey to Tokyo is a quest for true peace,
which is like Dante in Hakuchō's favorite anecdote of his journey to
Paris. And, just as Hakuchō noted of Dante, Toda was unable to
abandon life and remain in seclusion.

Toda says he must see his estranged wife Tomiko again; he has
been obsessed with thoughts of her for nearly twenty years. Suhara,
like Virgil, is ruled by reason and he points out that Toda's conception of Tomiko is an idealization, an illusion. Toda's beautiful
image of her would be destroyed, he warns, if he actually met her.
In this sense, Tomiko is Toda's Beatrice, whose ideal perfection, for
Hakuchō, is maintained at the expense of her humanity and
believability.

Above all, Toda is aware of death. He feels that only Tomiko can
grant peace before death. Meeting her will ease the pain of death.
Toward the close of the first act, Hakuchō begins to create ambiguity, an intentional blurring of the line between the reality of the
present and memories of the past. As Toda becomes increasingly
intense and vehement in his desire to see Tomiko, he notes how
much Kuniko resembles Tomiko at the time he married her. And
the handsome young man he recalls seeing her with on the streetcar
reminds him of his wife's young lover. Tomiko, like Kuniko, he
says, had tried to cover up her romance with denials and
inventions.

In the second act Tomiko arrives at the same study as in act one
to find Toda there alone. She has been accompanied by a young
man, who at times can be seen outside the window. Toda is soon in
tears; Tomiko tells him to forget the past. She has come only in
response to a desperate, pleading love letter from Toda.

They quarrel over who was really to blame for their separation,
but Hakuchō continues the process of ambiguity, of identification
of the present with the past. Although a realistic plot line has been
unfolding through most of the first act, it is soon thrown into
shadow by the gathering ambiguity.

Suhara's study, says Toda, is just like the study where he discovered his wife's adultery with the young man twenty years before. He became Tomiko's second husband, but he died of guilt over destroying Toda's marital happiness. Her third husband, however, looks just as Toda once did, not only in that he is a wealthy man of the world, but even physically.

Toda and Tomiko become more acrimonious. He complains that he is alone and abandoned; she accuses him of delighting in her suffering. She says it is none of his business when Toda asks if she is betraying her current husband the way she did him. Her young companion enters through the window. He is haughty and tells Tomiko that Toda stands in the way of their happiness; Toda feels he is the same young man who fled his study through the window twenty years before.

Tomiko tells the young man that Toda is the "shadow" of the man who stood in her way twenty years before. The young man throws Toda to the ground and kills him. He says that with Toda gone, they can enjoy perfect happiness, even if just for a day or but a moment.

In the third and final act, Suhara and Yoshiko are in the same study, reading Toda's torn letter. They seem unaware of the events of the second act; they think the letter must be from Ōmura to Kuniko, but she denies it. Kuniko's marriage appears to be off, but she is happy for Toda has opened her eyes. She feels Toda was especially sent to open her heart and tell her she was making a mistake. And Kuniko does not recall ever having the conversation with Ōmura that Toda reported seeing. Suhara and Yoshiko are unsure now of the author of the letter. They want to read it again, but have already burned it. On this note of uncertainty the play ends as the door bell rings noisily.

The past casts long shadows on the present. Current people and events become just faint, lingering images of what has gone before. These recurrent cycles of human activity suggest a dream-like perception of the timeless repetition of essentially the same human dramas.

II   The Joys of Life *(1924)*

Unlike *Shadows, The Joys of Life,* which Hakuchō wrote in April, 1924, was produced soon after by the Shingeki Kyōkai in October and again in December, 1924. The play was well received and praised by many, including the recent graduate of Tokyo Imperial University, Kawabata Yasunari, who called the playwright "Tensai Hakuchō," or Hakuchō the Genius.[4]

In *Joys of Life* a man is troubled by life and feels that his own younger sister, who is young and virginal, would be better off dead than alive. For when she grows up she will have to avenge her dead mother. The insane brother and virginal sister are of different mothers, and the girl's mother had been destroyed by the mother of the son. He feared the revenge of his younger sister and thus sought to kill her.

As it turns out, the sister ends up killing her older brother, but she is not discovered as another brother who has committed another murder confesses to his sister's crime as well. The sister looks at her dead brother after killing him and says that maybe now in death he has found happiness (or "joy"). At the end of the play the girl meets a philosopher to whom she makes her first confession of guilt; he concludes that she is now the same as her dead brother was, that is, tormented.

The somewhat incredible scene where the brother tries to strangle his sister only to be strangled by her instead calls to mind the ending of "Ghost Picture." There is also a philosophical link to "Illusion." Toyojirō, the older brother, wants to kill his sister in order to spare her the pain of existence. She, likewise, justifies her murder of him by saying that he is happier dead than alive, for in death he is free of the gloomy thoughts that obsessed him while alive.

In assuming that human existence is painful, Hakuchō is disagreeing with neither Buddhism nor Christianity; much of the thought of the former proceeds from the assumption that life is suffering, while the notion of the pain of temptation and sin is central to that of the latter. The point where Hakuchō may differ from Buddhist and Christian thought, especially the latter, is his apparent denial of life after death. As in "Illusion," death means the extinction of the self. The dead, Toyojirō in this case, are presumably happier than the living, not only because they are free of the cares of the world but also because they have ceased to exist. Kayoko, Toyojirō's sister, is left with her guilt, for as the play ends she expresses her confusion and sorrow.

The denial of the existence of life after death is never spelled out in *Joys of Life,* so that another more Christian interpretation of the play is possible. That is, that Toyojirō is a Christ-figure, for there are several references to such facts as that he submitted to death meekly and that he has also certainly forgiven his murderer. Like

Christ, he has expiated his sin through the sacrifice of his life.

Toyojirō forgives his murderer, Kayoko, because she murdered him out of the understandable human desire to avenge her dead mother. Kayoko's comments leading up to the murder show her suddenly aware of the human role she must play as an avenger of her abused late mother. This awareness transforms the innocent nineteen-year-old girl into a murderess. (This variation of the familiar Japanese theme of the vendetta runs throughout the play, and as such could offer yet another point of entry for interpretation.) Even with a Christian interpretation, there is no clear resolution in *Joys of Life,* no optimism in the ending, no positive note of self-discovery for Kayoko who is left behind with her guilt and her sin. Hakuchō leaves the sinner to live and suffer.

III   Beyond the Clouds *(1925)*

Beyond the Clouds is set in the Kambun Period (April, 1661 to September, 1673). It deals with the conversion to Christianity of a Kyushu youth. It is filled with attitudes and sentiments typical of Hakuchō.

The young man is attracted to Christianity through his admiration for the Bible. In it, he says, are ideas he cannot find in the Confucian *Analects.* Through the Bible he can discover the true dimensions of his "anima."[5]

The hero is hesitant to give in to the spell of the forbidden religion because he fears the wrath of the authorities, not toward himself but toward his ambitious brother. The hero does not fear death himself, for he is a descendant of the Shimabara defenders, the seventeenth-century Kyushu Christians who began a valiant but hopeless armed rebellion in the face of extreme poverty and government persecution of their religion. His spirituality is contrasted with the worldliness of his brother whose career he seeks to protect. Given Hakuchō's familiarity with the Bible, it is more than coincidence that the worldly brother is a scholar seeking government patronage.

There is an unnamed man, a mysterious character, who appears late at night and speaks persuasively of Christianity. He explains to the young hero, on one occasion before his final acceptance of Christianity, that the Shimabara defenders were the true victors in their struggle with the Japanese government. For, even though in 1638 the more than thirty thousand Shimabara Christians — men, women, and children — were finally slaughtered almost to a man, through their martyrdom they inherited the Kingdom of Heaven. The attitude of this character shows Hakuchō's understanding of fundamental Christian psychology.

Hakuchō does not make these Nagasaki Christians the subject of his play out of mere historical curiosity, nor for their exotic appeal to a contemporary Japanese audience. Rather, he chooses them because the extremity of their zeal makes them perfect illustrations of the power of the blind faith he always admired. Hakuchō even has the character who appears at night note that viewing the Shimabara defenders as a defeated army is the type of superficiality one would expect of a chronicler of war tales.[6]

Restraining Hakuchō's enthusiasm for blind faith in Christianity, however, is another familiar notion, namely Hakuchō's conception of omnipotent God as cruel and merciless in the light of the suffering of humanity. Resisting Christianity almost to the end, the hero exclaims to his brother the scholar, "And the cruelest of all is 'Deus' Who creates people at will for a life of suffering!... If 'Deus' does exist in the world, [the suffering] is on His head, and not my responsibility!"[7]

The young man is finally persuaded to accept Christianity by a vision, visible to himself but not to his brother. The fact of the hero's sudden faith is clearly established as the play ends, but there is still an ambiguous note. That is, Hakuchō draws a thin line in the audience's mind between blind faith and insanity. The audience has seen the apparition that converts the young man, but it is also possible to accept the common sense assessment of the scholar that there are no such things as spirits who visit the earth, and that his poor brother may indeed be mad. It goes almost without saying that this ambiguity reflects Hakuchō's own attitude for most of his life.

IV   The Nobunaga Trilogy *(1926)*

In early 1926 Hakuchō wrote what might be termed a Nobunaga trilogy. In February he published *Spring at Azuchi,* depicting the conqueror Oda Nobunaga in 1581, the year before his death. In March Hakuchō published *The End of Katsuyori,* dramatizing the last days, in early spring, 1582, of Takeda Katsuyori (1546–1582), whose Kōshū warriors were among the many vanquished by the seemingly invincible Nobunaga.

The contemporary comedy *The Man Who Isn't Welcome* appeared in May, but in June Hakuchō completed his dramatization of Nobunaga's last year with *Mitsuhide and Jōha*. It concerns the last weeks of Akechi Mitsuhide (1526–1582), who forced Nobunaga's suicide at the end of May only to become Hideyoshi's victim less than two weeks later.

This historical trilogy shows Hakuchō's unusual interest in Nobunaga; in 1953 he also wrote the story "Honnōji no Nobunaga" (Nobunaga of Honnōji Temple). Hakuchō may have been attracted to Nobunaga because of his well-known toleration of Christianity, which contrasts with the eventual fate of Christianity at the hands of the Tokugawas.[8] Another explanation for this interest in Nobunaga is the possibility that Hakuchō was a genealogical, but not blood, descendant of the famous warrior. Though the fact of that relationship may be impossible to verify, it does appear that Hakuchō heard such a story, which was probably an honored treasure of the family lore, from his mother from childhood and was under the impression that it was true.[9]

The thematic thrust of the three Nobunaga plays is the familiar Buddhist notion of life's impermanence. Classically, the fundamental evanescence of all life is illustrated best by the decline of the mighty. Nobunaga swept aside all opposition and held the power of life and death over all Japan until he was caught in a surprise attack on the lightly guarded Honnōji. Suddenly, his life and that of his heir Nobutada (1557–1582) became of no more consequence than those of the thousands Nobunaga had confidently and casually had slaughtered.

All three Nobunaga plays are imbued with the sense of life's transiency which was at the heart of the Buddhist philosophy of the medieval Japanese warrior. However, in *Spring at Azuchi,* Hakuchō contrasts Nobunaga not with another warrior, for example, a nobler or more loyal exemplar of the warrior ethic, but with a young Christian whose loyalty is to a Lord in Heaven.

Hakuchō's Nobunaga is arrogant, restless, and bloodthirsty, but he is aware of the certainty of his own death. He says he has no need of Buddha or Christ. He has only contempt for the Buddhist monks; and as for the Christian priests, he is interested only in the tales of their long, adventurous journeys to Japan. He feels that only the strong, such as himself, survive. Hakuchō illustrates the psychological strain of such purely rational determinism and self-reliance through Nobunaga's distressing tendency to order executions impulsively on the slightest pretext.

The young Christian, on the other hand, is presented as a hand-some, sensitive youth, who longs for the capitals of the West where men "live in harmony and like children of God" (*MHZ*, V, 221). He is cut down senselessly by Nobunaga, who discovers him in innocent conversation with one of the young women attendants from Nobunaga's Azuchi Castle. Nobunaga murders them both on the spot; the young man shouts the name "Jesus Christ" as he is killed.

In *The End of Katsuyori* there are many well-drawn minor characters who present several corresponding contrasts, but the most important couple to our discussion is Katsuyori and his wife. Katsuyori is the consummate example of the romantic ideal of the Japanese warrior. He is concerned, above all, with worldly honor.

It is a cruel predicament in which the heroic Katsuyori finds him-self. His allies have betrayed him and even his best Kōshū warriors are deserting him to save themselves. He is properly fatalistic. He may lack the genius of his father, Takeda Shingen (1521–1573), but he will doggedly play out his appointed role to preserve the honor of the family name even in the face of the relentless pursuit of Nobunaga and Tokugawa Ieyasu, among others.

In proper fashion Katsuyori is aware of the sad waste of his life and of the inevitability of his end. Although resigned to his own fate, he seeks nobly to save the life of his devoted wife by delivering her into safe hands before his time is played out. She is equal to her role, too, however, and convinces him of her determination to accompany him to the grave out of both love and duty.

He indulges in sweet self-pity as his end approaches. And he strikes the proper, resonant historical note by comparing his fate to that of the quintessential romantic idealization of the Japanese warrior mystique — the tragic fate of the twelfth-century Heike clan.

It would not be Hakuchō if there were not a bit more than the familiar, however. That is, Katsuyori's wife is devoutly Buddhist. Her strength more than matches that of her brave, determined hus-band; her Buddhist faith is the source of her courage. She prays to Yakushi[10] that she and her husband may be born on the same lotus flower in paradise. She describes the purple cloud on which they will make their ascent to paradise.

As the play ends, Katsuyori rejoins his staunchest remaining fol-lower and announces that he has ended his wife's life. But he con-fesses that even as he slit her throat he was unable to see the purple cloud she had spoken of seeing, that would carry them to their lotus seat. In hopeless desperation he postpones his own suicide and joins his savage follower in a final combat to carry a few of the enemy with them before they die.

Katsuyori is incapable of belief and is, thus, unable to see the purple cloud and unable to die. He retreats into the bravado of the warrior and rushes off in hopes of a sudden, unexpected death. His wife, however, provides yet another example of the power of blind faith. She is the medieval Buddhist true believer for whose psychology Hakuchō expresses his great admiration in "On Dante" the following year. Her kingdom is in "the world beyond," on a lotus perch in paradise; she has no fear of death.

In his third Nobunaga drama, *Mitsuhide and Jōha,* Hakuchō is the most successful in creating the twilight atmosphere of mystery usually associated with medieval Japanese warrior dramas. He evokes this mood by setting the entire play at night and through dramatic tension between Mitsuhide and Satomura Jōha (1524–1602), a *renga* (linked verse) poet under the patronage of Nobunaga and reluctant poetry companion of Mitsuhide.

The play consists of two acts of three scenes each. Scene one, act one, is set on the night of May 28 on Mt. Atago. Mitsuhide and Jōha are composing poetry by dim light. Jōha is perplexed by Mitsuhide's questions about the depth of the ditch outside the Honnōji temple, but is forced to agree to accompany Mitsuhide to Tamba.

Scene two is again at night, as they travel by torchlight. They are off to kill Nobunaga, although Jōha is still unaware of the plot. The third scene is in the evening twilight of June 1, after the successful attack on Nobunaga and his heir. Jōha has slipped away from the camp; Mitsuhide stuns his followers by revealing his resolve to conquer all of Japan.

Scene one, act two, is another twilight evening, that of June 10. Jōha returns to camp, only to be tied up by Mitsuhide's followers. They suspect Jōha of being a spy for the forces loyal to the late Nobunaga, despite Mitsuhide's warm reception of him. The second scene takes place in a dimly lighted room in Mitsuhide's encampment. Jōha is tied up and forgotten. However, he is able to convince three wandering swordsmen that he had come to Mitsuhide to avenge Nobunaga's death; they untie him on the promise of reward.

The final scene is also at night, on a country road in Ogurusu

where, after the defeat of his forces by those of Hideyoshi, Akechi
Mitsuhide meets his end at the hands of local peasants. Jōha and
his three benefactors hide when they hear approaching horsemen.
It is Mitsuhide and a few followers; their horses are tired. Suddenly
a spear from a nearby thicket pierces Mitsuhide's side. Jōha and
Mitsuhide look at one another in the moonlight. Mitsuhide moves
off slowly.

They are poet and lord; Jōha is a helpless observer of the pathos
of Mitsuhide's life. Jōha is berated by Mitsuhide's men for being
merely a poet, worthless in times of war. Mitsuhide, on the other
hand, is a man of action; the tragic irony of his story is the fact that
he tries to control his own fate. Both are suited to the prevailing
darkness of the play. Mitsuhide exhibits a gloomy determination in
the face of the blackest fate.

As they write poems in the dim light, Mitsuhide recognizes
Jōha's role as an observer. Jōha is called an owl, whose gaze,
Mitsuhide notes, can penetrate the darkness and read the hopeless-
ness of his fate although it is the darkest night Mitsuhide has ever
seen and the wind has extinguished their lamp.

Mitsuhide and Jōha are companions, but hardly true friends. An
effective aspect of this play is that both men are made to seem isolated. Mitsuhide is set apart by the absurdity of his initial grandiose
ambition and, finally, by the solitude of his miserable death.

Jōha lives in an intellectual isolation as a sensitive but cautious[11]
poet forced to pick his way among the reckless warriors on all sides.
Mitsuhide does not divulge his plans of conquest to Jōha. Jōha
exists merely to soothe him with poetry or be killed. To the warrior,
the poet is of use but dispensable. Still, only the poet's awareness,
his owl's eyes that pierce the darkness, sees the total horror of
Mitsuhide's life.

Jōha is merely a perceptive but powerless witness to events, but
Mitsuhide, sensing his understanding, is convinced that Jōha has
the magic power to control their destiny. His warriors are also
unable to accept Jōha as he is; they make him a scapegoat for their
defeat. They say his foolish poetry distracted their lord and they tie
up Jōha. Seeing the bound Jōha, Mitsuhide imagines himself fet-
tered and helpless.

Jōha witnesses the fatal thrust and knows that only he has perceived the frightening truth of Mitsuhide's adventure. Only he has
understood the desperation at the heart of Mitsuhide's ambition
and abandon.

Mitsuhide is, thus, given a different dimension, if not more depth or a more sympathetic treatment, than in the *kabuki* play *Ehon Taikō-ki* (The Picture Book of the Taikō).[12] In both the Hakuchō and *kabuki* plays Mitsuhide is seen as a figure of great ambition but limited intelligence who rushes blindly into the jaws of his fate. Only when firmly in their grip does Mitsuhide dumbly recognize the inevitability and pity of his failure. However, whereas Hakuchō's inclusion of the intelligent Jōha witnessing Mitsuhide's death provides a full explication of the futility of his life, the *kabuki* play merely ends with the premonition of the extremity of his miserable death.

V Iwami Jūtarō *(1935)*

Iwami Jūtarō has no overtly Christian or strictly religious theme. However, it does contain a familiar attitude toward divinity. Iwami is a warrior-hero who happens upon a remote village that has been the victim of a cruel "god" (*kami*) for several years. Each year the demonic *kami* has been forcing the villagers to offer him a young maiden of his choosing for him to devour.

Iwami expresses his inability to comprehend a god that would assume the form of a monster and commit such acts of cruelty. Iwami, of course, drives away the monster-god and saves the maidens of the village.

Iwami is identified with "human justice" (*seigi jindō*); it is the source of his "strength of a thousand men." The innate goodness of the human hero is pitted against the malevolent perversity of the deity. In fact, the deity explains his cruel actions of the previous years as merely a way to dispel his boredom. This recalls somewhat Hakuchō's view of Nobunaga and the notion that man cannot bear the quiet of peaceful inactivity.

The monstrous deity says he is not sure himself whether he is a god or a demon, and furthermore he does not recall any promise to the villagers to act just as human beings conceive a god should act.[13] The implication is that he is merely what he is, that human beings conceive of him as a god or as a monster to suit their own needs.

Hakuchō raises such stimulating questions in *Iwami Jūtarō,* but prefers to sublimate them to the telling of his heroic tale. For a Hakuchō play, *Iwami* offers considerable visual, purely theatrical possibilities with the deity in a monster's costume and the brave

Iwami with a large placard on his chest proclaiming *"sennin-riki,"* "the strength of a thousand men." When the deity concedes defeat in his fight with Iwami, the sign is changed to read *"mannin-riki,"* "the strength of ten thousand men"; as the play closes, Iwami leads the maiden he has just rescued in a round of yelling *"banzai."* It is not surprising that this play is one of those still performed.

VI   Capture the Angel *(1947)*

Capture the Angel was published in December, 1947, and performed the following summer. Hakuchō utilizes the form of the drama with more effect than in any of his other plays. Because of the bitter lessons of the war, although avoiding total cynicism, Hakuchō shows an increased sophistication in his ironic handling of the supernatural. Hakuchō combines his usual thematic interest in the hereafter with current, almost topical, concerns, so that he speaks to his contemporaries in a direct way he had rarely achieved for decades.

Capture the Angel is set in the mountains "in a place like Karui-zawa." The characters include: the professor (about forty years old), his wife (about thirty), a neighbor (a man about thirty), and a couple of angels.

The professor and his wife are relaxing outdoors after a morning of gardening when their neighbor appears for a visit. Judging from comments about the scarcity of food and the fact that the professor of history and his wife have been raising their own food for two years, the time is the grim early days of the postwar period. As their neighbor says, it is a time when everyone is hard of hearing, for when you ask someone for a second bowl of rice, he says, "oh, is one bowl all you wanted," and puts the rice away.

The three characters reveal much about themselves as they talk idly. The neighbor, a petty government official, is preoccupied with wealth and possessions. He has no spiritual dimension, nor any cultural or intellectual attainments. For example, he boasts that he knows a black marketeer who is, for some reason, awed by poetry. He tries to convince the professor to impress the black marketeer with his scholarly air and reputation. He is certain his shady friend would advance him money to finance some great academic project.

The professor is pessimistic and skeptical by nature. His studies and his farming seem equally futile to him. His wife, however, is more positive, although ultimately her philosophy seems somehow muddled. Early in the play she says that people literally reap what they sow; that is, they can expect no divine help or intervention in life. Later, however, upset by her husband's characteristic skepticism, she says, with some conviction, that faith can move mountains. They discuss this idea lightly, the men telling her to try moving one of the area mountains with her faith.

At this point she astonishes them by assuming the manner of a seer or medium. She gazes at the blue sky where a winged angel appears. She begins to speak with the voice of the angel. Through her the angel tells them of the joy and nobility of labor. The angel tells them to endure their poverty and rid themselves of vulgar desires. The angel says people get the happiness they deserve and should be satisfied with that happiness.

The neighbor does not actually see the angel and the professor is deliberately vague about whether or not he sees him. But the neighbor says he is not satisfied with his portion of happiness. The angel answers that, in that case, he will fly him away on the back of an eagle to a far-off paradise. The neighbor says he is not interested, so the wife uses her bamboo broom to chase the angel away. After the angel disappears into the sky, they joke about how plain and uninspiring their angel was compared to those they have seen in Western paintings.

Soon the professor also assumes the pose of a diviner and another angel, his angel, appears and speaks through the professor himself. He offers to take them to a fabulous place in the sky where supernatural beings assemble and all is music and enchantment. "Once you have entered this world," says the angel, "you will never want to leave" (*MHZ,* V, 341). But both the professor and his neighbor agree that they would be afraid to go to a world from which they could never return to this one. This time the professor takes the broom and chases the angel away.

They talk over what has happened and how easily they chased the angels away. The neighbor did not see any angels himself, but when *his* angel appears, he will capture him alive and put him in a cage. He will take the captive angel to Tokyo and make a sideshow of him. They could all get rich, he says. The professor can give the introductions and his wife can interpret what the angel says.

The neighbor says he will return with a cage tomorrow. The professor is also enthusiastic. He will begin research on angels at once. He has done historical research for many years, but this is the first time he has felt his research would prove worthwhile. His wife at first doubts that an angel would allow himself to be captured. The neighbor reminds her that the angel had said that only with a spirit of adventure could they find happiness. He argues that the capturing of the angel will be their adventure.

Convinced, the wife gets busy converting their farm implements into instruments with which to catch an angel. As the play opened, the professor and his wife had spoken of the need for a change in their monotonous and futile lives. As the play ends, they agree that that change has come.

The humor of *Capture the Angel* is a refreshing change from Hakuchō's usually more serious style. Also of significance is Hakuchō's comment upon both human nature in general and postwar Japanese life in particular. He implies that man is avaricious by nature. He must satisfy his physical needs before he worries, if at all, about his spiritual needs. In a time of privation such as the mid-1940s these "truths" became obvious. Also, the rough treatment and exploitation of the angel seem to capture the spirit of the Occupation Period in Japan. There was no time to worry about the other world or afterlife, for the demands of this world and this life were too pressing. As a result, it was a time when energy and resourcefulness were rewarded.

Hakuchō is making an ironic statement about the crass materialism and lack of spirituality of his contemporary countrymen. Still, prewar Shintō mysticism had been almost thoroughly discredited; it was hardly the time to trust angels.

VII   Ejima Ikushima *(1953)*

Ejima (1681–1741) was the senior lady-in-waiting in charge of the other ladies-in-waiting in the inner palace during the time of the seventh Tokugawa shogun, the boy Ietsugu (1709–1716). Ejima's secret visits to the *kabuki* performances of the Yamamura-za (Yamamura Troupe) and her affair with the actor Ikushima became a sensational scandal of the Edo Period.

In their typical indiscriminate, scathing fashion the Tokugawa authorities punished not only Ejima and Ikushima, but everyone associated in any way with Ejima's indiscretions. In all, more than fifteen hundred people received various punishments, including even execution. Ikushima was banished to a distant island and Ejima to a remote area of mountainous Nagano Prefecture.[14]

Hakuchō's play focuses entirely on Ejima. It was performed in November, 1953, and again in November, 1954; it appeared in

Gunzō in January, 1953. The first act establishes the rural isolation of Ejima's exile. She is surrounded by farmers and other rustics; the only man of interest is Bunnoshin, a wealthy townsman who bought his way into a position as one of the "samurai" who escorted her into exile.

Bunnoshin declares his devotion to the beautiful Ejima, but at first she is adamant in her resolve to live a penitent life with her rosary and the Lotus Sutra. He wants to see the dagger Ikushima gave her, but she says it must never leave her person. He is insistent and she drives him back threatening to stab him. Then, in a sudden change of heart, she shows him the knife, which proves to be a harmless stage prop. Hakuchō closes the first act by introducing the familiar theme of ambiguity, in this case confusion and trans-ference of identities. In *Ejima* it is handled with a light touch, and its meaning within the play is more obvious than usual.

EJIMA: All of a sudden I'm growing fond of you. I don't know whether you'll believe me when I tell you, but I've noticed that your face is a lot like Ikushima's. At first I didn't think so, but slowly I've come to. Especially when I frightened you with the toy dagger a moment ago, you were exactly like Ikushima. I wonder if there is such a thing as a man or woman who looks like no one else. Before you came here, I was drowsing and happened to hear a farmer from the village saying that if he cleaned up a little he'd look like Ikushima. That may've been the joking of a provincial, but I don't think my regarding you as Ikushima is a foolish delusion. I think that in fact Ikushima may have purposely changed his own face, form, and voice into those of a wealthy merchant called Bunno-shin and appeared here. It's something actors often do on the stage. If we remove the mask and reveal the true identity, wouldn't we have Ikushima in the flesh?

BUNNOSHIN: You mean that Ikushima longed for you so much that he changed himself into me and accompanied you here. Then, please believe that. I would cherish that thought all my life.

EJIMA: Yes, if there really are such things.

BUNNOSHIN: If there really are such things. (*MHZ,* V, 351–352)

As in *Shadows* thirty years before, with the second act the "plot" per se is thrown out the window. Bunnoshin, Ejima, the farmers, a samurai, a doctor, and others are gathered for a meal. They are in Edo Period costume, but their speech is modern and their fare like that of wartime evacuees. They are a lively, humor-ous bunch which Bunnoshin identifies as the remnants of the

Yamamura-za. (The farmers quip that they'd better dress up if they're going to be actors.) Hakuchō, however, identifies them as the Sokai-za (Evacuee Troupe).

Most of their humor is at the expense of the Edo samurai cult and the Tokugawa inner palace where women are kept from male companionship, restrained by etiquette, and forced to live in boredom. They all admire Ejima's courage in defying the authorities; they are all fascinated by her. She defends desire as natural; she performs for them. They all give little performances; there is applause from unseen spectators.

Earlier they were addressed by an offstage voice; now there is a song from offstage. It is a lyrical, sensual song of the soothing sound of waves, two perfect bodies, the rays of the sun playing upon naked bodies in the sand, birds flying about to sing Ejima's praises, and the fact that men's eyes were made to gaze at her. This expression of total inhibition from social mores and of the natural fulfillment of physical desire merely rephrases the dreams of Tomoe and Toyomura in "Nightmare," thirty-three years before.

In her song Ejima says that people are as ugly as rotten persimmons in her eyes; she cannot bear the stench. There is applause from the unseen spectators, but the members of the Evacuee Troupe feel insulted by her declarations. Bunnoshin tries to calm them with the reminder that they are all just actors. It's just a play, he says; there's no need to be angry.

The samurai, the buffoon of the play, thinks they should perform *The 47 Rōnin,* but Ejima is, naturally, opposed to glorifications of the cruel samurai ethic. As they quarrel, Bunnoshin himself becomes angry at the warrior, for he feels he is insulting his Ejima. Now it is the samurai who must remind Bunnoshin that it is just a play and that he is merely speaking his lines.

Nevertheless, the argument continues. Bunnoshin recounts how much money he has spent to bring about a show called *Ejima Ikushima.* Finally, the samurai draws his sword, but Bunnoshin succeeds in stabbing him with the samurai's own weapon. The warrior falls; the unseen spectators applaud. Ejima says now it's starting to look like a real play; it doesn't seem like a real play unless someone is killed on stage. But, Bunnoshin protests, it looks like this guy is really dead; it was a real sword. It can't be helped, Ejima answers; buy your way out of it. That, she then announces, concludes this performance of the Evacuee Troupe.

Hakuchō is seeking the play within a play. Breaking down the conventional barriers between actors and audience, he tries to jar the audience's sense of reality, even if only momentarily. The actors are easily identifiable as characters in a somewhat conventional historical drama in the first act, but in act two there is a confusion of the historical and the contemporary. With the distance between actor and audience thus shortened, Hakuchō then has the actors appear to be ordinary people acting as actors acting.

The audience always knows they are actors, of course, so the effect of this ambiguity is neither jarring nor dramatic; rather, the effect is ironic. The actors move in and out of their roles, and a puzzling blurring of character identification results. Hakuchō is his most purely theatrical in this work, for the possibilities of theater itself become the message. We have seen some thematic links of *Ejima* to other Hakuchō works, but in this play at least what impresses most is not so much what is said as how it is said.

Consequently, act three is merely a brief appendage, performed outside the curtain. Bunnoshin explains that he is going back to Edo. He will never forget Ejima or the others, but it took nearly all his money to buy his way out of the murder and he has, in short, had enough. He will never return to the mountains and never see Ejima again.

Hakuchō adds this little farewell as a way of reassuring his audience and restoring their sense of reality. Although it hardly seems necessary, it is as if he were admitting that he was only fooling them before. On the other hand, this return to the realistic has the effect of adding further to the confusion.

The play is designated as "intended as a farce," and it is appropriately light and humorous. The lingering absurdity of the puzzle of just what transpired in the second act reflects Hakuchō's notion in the 1950s of the inability of literature to provide answers to fundamental philosophical questions. Without even the slightest hope of such unlikely information, literature becomes what Hakuchō had perhaps always feared it ultimately is: merely literature.

VIII   A Death-like Peace *(1957)*

The one-act play *A Death-like Peace* appeared in January, 1957, and was performed by the Haiyūza theatrical troupe, April 6 to 21, 1957. Its three scenes take place in the quiet "enchanting" suburban home of Toyozawa Hisashi (about fifty years old) and his wife Sato ("past 30"). They live in middle-class comfort, served by their maid Matsu; their custom is to engage in long somewhat philosophical after-dinner discussions by the dim glow of candlelight.

Hisashi evaluates everything and everyone in terms of money. He is to receive a large stock dividend and is feeling pleased with the comfort, calm, and security his financial well-being brings. Sato, on the other hand, views their uneventful lives as a death-like peace. She feels Hisashi should risk their money, that failure only means suicide or a life of poverty, both preferable alternatives to the boredom of their current lives.

Throughout the play, the dialogue between Hisashi, Sato, and sometimes Matsu, becomes a litany of several thoughts, which are repeated and freely associated by all three characters. This chain of ideas includes: ennui; death-like peace, described as true peace; Hisashi's desire for money which contrasts with Sato's desire for foolhardy adventure; Hisashi's preference for the shadows of candlelight versus Sato's frustrated longing for brilliant light; bewitching and possession of both Sato and Matsu by foxes and badgers, both common agents of the supernatural in Japanese oral tradition; folk notions such as burning pine branches to smoke into true form the fox who has bewitched a woman; dances by Matsu while secretly wearing Sato's clothes and seeming, to some extent, to assume her identity; the notion of a play within a play; and an awareness of life's evanescence, of the inevitability of death.

In the initial scene Matsu seems bewitched as she sings for Hisashi and Sato in the candlelight, first of an abandoned child and death, then of her bewitchment. Her second lyrical narration occupies the entirety of the brief second scene. It is set in the same room as the first but on the following morning; Matsu wears her mistress's clothes and seems to become Sato.

The third scene is in the same room but once more at night. Hisashi has deposited his dividend money and is explaining how their value as human beings has increased in proportion to the increase in their bank account. His wife greets this sarcastically. Still, when an old, close friend of Hisashi comes begging for a modest loan to pay his wife's hospital bills and save his household from ruin, Sato tricks him. She sends him away with a packet of colored paper which he assumes is money. She has deceived him, she tells her husband, "to preserve our deathly peace."

The play closes with Matsu's third and final incantation. Its symbolic language speaks of the futility of human desire. There is an awareness of man's true, helpless state and a desperate resolve to laugh in the face of despair. This new knowledge is derived from a transcendent, or supernatural, experience. The supernatural is presented in terms of bewitching, and is thus intellectually on about the level of Hakuchō's favorite play *Peony Lantern.* However, within the context of *A Death-like Peace,* Hakuchō comes as close as he ever has to evoking his notion of the transcendent. And, in Matsu's final lines, there is a link with the sentiments of the final paragraphs of his "On Dante," nearly thirty years before.

MATSU: Have I given myself away? Then I haven't learned enough.

If only I could make gold look like leaves and leaves like gold, I'd not care what happens in the world.

Laughing and crying are the same thing. If they are the same, laugh through life!

I had a dream last night.

I dreamed of a bride.

A beautiful bride.

A bride like a queen.

There were voices here and there.

Perhaps that bride was I.

But, although every bride must have a groom, there was no sign of a groom.

A bride without a groom.

A bride all by herself.

I wept. I sobbed.

When I awoke, there were tears in my eyes.

My cheeks and pillow were wet with tears.

Could I cry such tears? My little room was wet with tears.

What a fool I am! Damn!

Shall I burn my room?

In the dead of night.

Turn this area into a great expanse of burnt ruins and the city will be but a field.

The bride will become a maid; the millionaire a penniless beggar.

So laugh! Those who cry are fools!

Burn and dry

My foolish tears.

SATO: I'm frightened. Matsu's face is as frightening as if she were possessed.

Matsu puts on even more of an act that our caller did.

MATSU: I'm sorry.   (Curtain) (*MHZ,* V, 374)

CHAPTER 7

Death

IN the view of the eminent Protestant theologian Kitamori Kazō, it was Hakuchō's fear of death that led him to Christianity. What was impressed upon Hakuchō by Uchimura Kanzō was that every Christian must bear his cross. Every Christian had to have resolve in the face of death. Hakuchō was unable to accept death, and his realization of this forced him in his essential honesty to abandon Christianity.

Nonetheless, Hakuchō never completely deserted the Christian sphere, but continued, in Kitamori's words, to orbit the faith like a satellite. Kitamori notes that in discussing the difference between the Buddhist and Christian approaches to salvation, Hakuchō once said that whereas Buddhism takes one in gently, Christianity is severe and makes its converts shoulder their crosses and go off to battle. He sees Hakuchō's frequent reference to Christianity's severity as a result of his own religious suffering in trying to accept Christianity.

Kitamori claims to have predicted for many years before Hakuchō's death that he would one day return to the fold and to have surmised that the most likely time for Hakuchō's reaffirmation of Christianity would be as death approached. To Kitamori a constant preoccupation throughout the sixty years of Hakuchō's thought from his early twenties until his death is this fear of death. This fear led him initially to Christianity and then, in a sense, forced him away when he realized his inability to overcome it in the way he felt was required of a true Christian.

What Hakuchō wanted to write about more than anything was the ugly spectacle of man consumed with desire as though death were not lying before him. His first consideration was not literary skill but the depiction of the puzzle of human existence.[1]

Hakuchō left behind four brief portraits of death, stories written upon the deaths of his father, mother, eldest younger brother, and third younger brother, respectively. With his father's death he learned firsthand of both the awful physical pain that often accompanies death and the body's tenacious clinging to life.

Through the death of his mother Hakuchō was shown that although death can be relatively painless and "easy," it can involve intolerable loneliness. The death of his first brother demonstrated the attraction of serenity in the face of death as well as the blessings and comfort of even a reluctant baptism. His third younger brother's death was a reminder to Hakuchō of the absurdity of attachment to life and the futility of artistic aspirations.

The question concerning Hakuchō in these four "fictional essays" (for that is what they are) is how to die. In observing the processes or aftermath of these deaths Hakuchō always has in mind his own death.

First, there is the question of ceremony. Hakuchō recognizes that human rituals surrounding death are as much for the benefit and solace of the survivors as for that of the departed. At the same time, however, participation in and acceptance of religious ritual can bring the dying person a release from his fear of death. It is only through religious ritual, which gives meaning to death, that death truly becomes a part of life. The dying party is participating in the lives of those around him until the very end. In so doing, his death imparts meaning to the actions of himself and those attending him.

For Hakuchō, the choice was between Buddhist and Christian ceremony. The former Hakuchō associated with an older, pre-Meiji view of life. On the other hand, Christianity was, not surprisingly, an appropriately "modern" and more appealing philosophy for Hakuchō, who was educated in the atmosphere of Meiji enlightenment. Thus, as we have already seen in other contexts, it was a case of the "old" Buddhism versus the "new" Christianity.

Second, the four portraits of death describe a corresponding tension between Hakuchō's familial and social ties to Honami and the pull upon his priorities of his life in Tokyo. Each death in the family brings a hurried train ride back to Honami. Each death snips one more strand linking Hakuchō to his Honami origins and all they represent. Each death brings further isolation and loneliness which, as he learned from the loneliness of his mother's declining years, makes the fear of death all the more acute.

Increasing awareness of death brings an increased need for the strength to face it. In Tokyo Hakuchō was alone, except for his wife, waiting for his own hour to come. The appropriateness of Christianity for the Meiji-educated Hakuchō, the lessening of his ties to the Buddhist rituals of Honami, the example of his first brother's deathbed baptism in Honami, and the strain of his increasing age and isolation make Hakuchō's return to Christianity understandable.

Finally, Hakuchō speaks of death as the "ultimate reality." Paradoxically, death is both an answer to Hakuchō's "puzzle of human existence" and, at the same time, the most perplexing aspect of that very riddle. In the faces of the dead Hakuchō sees more "reality" than in the faces of the living.

I 'Spring This Year'' (1934)

Hakuchō's father Uraji died in Honami on April 10, 1934; Hakuchō's story commemorating his death appeared in *Waseda Bungaku* in June, 1934. Hakuchō's biographers accept "Spring This Year" as a factual account of the passing of Hakuchō's father. Still, the story is presented as, more than anything, simply a story. Hakuchō's father is the "aged head of a venerable family," Hakuchō himself is the old man's first son Ichirō, and Hakuchō's first brother, the noted scholar of Japanese classical literature Masamune Atsuo, is the second son Jirō.

Hakuchō was never, and certainly is not today, a widely read, or "popular," writer. His readership was drawn from that of such journals as the *Chūō Kōron* and *Waseda Bungaku*. His readers could know that this work of "fiction," or *shōsetsu,* "Spring This Year," was a factual account of his own experiences. However, by "disguising" himself as Ichirō, Atsuo as Jirō, and so on, his and his family's personal experiences become those of "others." That is, what would have been referred to as "I" or "mine" becomes "he" or "his." Hakuchō achieves a necessary distance from his obviously personal subject, the death of his father.

Discussions of narrative point of view may seem a musty critical approach to some of late, but it remains true, nonetheless, that through the use of the third person Hakuchō's thoughts on both death and his father's pain in death become the anxiety and suffering of all men. The paradoxical contrast of the body's mindless tenacity versus the solitary pain and universality of death is the point of Hakuchō's "fictional essay" "Spring This Year."

Hakuchō describes how his father, the "aged head of a venerable family," has survived ten years since being stricken with palsy. But now, on the verge of death, his mind remains clear, his hearing exceptional, his urination regular, and his heart strong. Only his stomach is weak. In Hakuchō's words, his stomach is dying, while the rest of him goes on living.

Finally, he can no longer even drink water. He is unafraid of death itself, only of a painful death. Still, he has spent a month in misery unable to eat. To Hakuchō, although existence is marked by suffering, man instinctively, but perplexingly, clings to life. This is the "lesson" of the death of Masamune Uraji.

When Ichirō imagined the pain of living and the pain of dying of his ill, elderly father, he felt it to be the pain of all people. At such a time as this, even the opiate of skillfully contrived religions was of no use whatsoever to his sick old father.

Because of the difficulty of speaking his father had taken to writing in the air with his finger to communicate his innermost feelings to those attending him.

"I want to die but I can't."

His hands now resembled those of a dead man. He gazed at them there side by side before his eyes. "My whole body's dried up," he said in a faint voice. Just as he said, his entire body was rough and dry. Still, it seemed his mind would remain active until the last drop of his blood was expended. (*MHZ*, III, 446)

II   *"Early Summer This Year"* (1943)

Hakuchō's mother Mine died on April 25, 1942. "Early Summer This Year" appeared in *Yakumo* in June, 1943. It takes up where "Spring This Year" leaves off. However, Hakuchō makes no attempt this time to create fictional distance between himself and his subject matter. He uses a first-person narrative for the story of his mother's sudden, relatively painless but lonely death. "Early Summer" is indeed an "essay," but it is "fictional" only in the sense that it is a Japanese *shōsetsu*, which term covers a wide range of forms, as we have seen.

With his mother's death there seemed to be no one willing to live in and take care of the Masamune family home, the "last remaining old-style house in the village" (*MHZ*, IV, 99). Hakuchō, his brothers, and his sisters are all loathe to see the family home abandoned, but none wants to be the one to return to Honami. For, with its factories lining the shore of the bay, it is no longer the genteel village of their youth. As Hakuchō puts it in his characteristic way, they would rather brave "the anonymity of the dust (*jin'ai*) of the city" (*MHZ*, IV, 103).

Hakuchō had read the relief from suffering in the visage of his dead father, who had no religion. But, paradoxically, he perceived no such release in the expression of his dead mother, who had immersed herself in Buddhist ritual soon after losing her husband.

> I could not see the tranquillity in my mother's face that I was able to see on the face of my dead father. There was no reason to expect any trace of suffering; literally, she had simply died of old age. Still, I was struck by something like the shadow of death itself. Will that shadow be inscribed in my memory forever as the face of my dead mother? All the philosophy and religion, poetry and prose of my years of study were, in short, empty words. My mother's dead body now revealed to me the ultimate reality. (*MHZ*, IV, 100)

In "Early Summer This Year" the ever-present problem of religion is discussed, specifically, in terms of the suitability of different ceremonies for Hakuchō's own funeral. The significance usually ascribed to ceremony in Japan is, no doubt, partly responsible for Hakuchō's concern here. But, more importantly, the selection of religion is a question of choice, a decision determined, in Hakuchō's case, by attitudes developed mostly during his Meiji youth.

> Eight years ago, at the time of my father's death, a group of women of various ages, skilled at sutra reading, gathered on several occasions to exclaim in chorus the prayers of Kūkai to the spirit of the deceased or to chant to the accompaniment of a gong. This time, too, we decided to invite them and have them pray for the repose of the deceased. When we were all in attendance and listening attentively, I was moved by the sadness of their recitations. Suddenly, however, I imagined myself following my parents someday and embarking upon my journey from this world to the next amid the send-off of such gongs and such meager elegies. What an odious thought; definitely something would feel lacking. (*MHZ*, IV, 103)

III   *"Autumn of This Year" (1959)*

Hakuchō's eldest younger brother Atsuo died in November, 1958. As had become Hakuchō's custom, this became the subject of his "Autumn of This Year," which soon appeared in *Chūō Kōron,* January, 1959.

Like "Early Summer This Year," "Autumn" is more of a straightforward essay than fiction, but it is an essay *à clef.* That is, Hakuchō relates events factually but refers to people concerned by Roman letters, a practice frequently encountered in modern Japanese fiction. Atsuo is "A," Hakuchō's eccentric third brother Ritsushi is "R," and so on. Thus, the "key" to actual identities is an obvious one.

The atmosphere of the "story" is reminiscent of the traditional Japanese literary genre, the *zuihitsu,* in which the author seems to be, as the term literally implies, "following the brush," wherever it leads him. The brush, that is, the work of literature, on the one hand, has a will of its own, but, at the same time, is always ulti-mately a servant of the author's thoughts and intentions. This implies that, due to the nature of the medium, in this case writing, art never takes shape exactly as the artist intends. Conversely, how-ever, a work of art can never create itself. As Hakuchō maintained in his debate on Tolstoy with Kobayashi Hideo in 1936, art always springs from and, to a great extent, remains subject to "real life."

To Japanese readers, "Autumn of This Year" is "fiction," or at least certainly *shōsetsu,* in the sense that Hakuchō uses the real-life events of his brother's life as a springboard to the world of his fantasies (in a favorite Hakuchō term, his *kūsō,* that is, "fancies" or "daydreams") of his own death. The balance is generally tilted toward description of the facts of his brother's death, which is "real," not *kūsō,* but the selection of facts and, above all, the almost lyrical language make this essay "fictional," at least within the context of Japanese attitudes toward fiction. For example, Hakuchō begins his fictional essay as follows:

October is a good month but always rainy. Whether for travel or staying at home the most pleasant time is from about November. How will I spend autumn of this year? November 1, 1958: I left the house intending to attend the arts festival being celebrated at the Kabukiza, and then drop in at the radio station. (*MHZ,* IV, 584)

Hakuchō's routine, leisurely taping session at the radio station is interrupted by a phone call telling him of his brother's critical ill-ness; there follows the familiar long train ride to Honami to try to arrive before it is too late. This time, unlike his mother's death six-teen years earlier, he arrives in time.

A (Atsuo) is lucid, but unimpressed with the fact of so many visi-tors. His pylorus is obstructed; he has cancer but does not know it, so he still seems to have hopes for recovery.

In his brother's presence, Hakuchō finds himself thinking about the reality of a final farewell to a dying loved one. Is one of necessity struck by sentimental and moving things to say at such a time, or are such assumptions merely the fabrications of poets and novelists? As always, there is the blurring of the distinction between art and reality, the confusion he utilized effectively in many of his plays.

One difference between "Autumn" and Hakuchō's two earlier portraits of death is his attitude toward Honami. Now he describes himself entering the ancient family home "like an intruder" (*MHZ*, IV, 587). Clearly the ties to the psychology and ways of Homani have about reached the breaking point. Hakuchō wonders specifically about whether he should be buried there. His native village is a suitable spot for A, the scholar of classical literature, but not apparently for the modern intellectual Hakuchō.

Relatives are pressing for A to be baptized before he dies. In the end, he does accept baptism. To Hakuchō, while in Honami, this baptism seems forced upon his brother, by circumstances as much as anything. Still, Hakuchō feels the baptism is of great significance to himself.

I felt as if even a forced baptism would ease the pain of death. Although I was certain they would conduct Buddhist services in the nearby temple according to the customs of generations of our ancestors, when I thought of A entrusting things to the mercy of Christ in his last moments, I felt it might be of somewhat more effect in easing my own life and death sorrows than those of A himself. (*MHZ*, IV, 590)

Even Atsuo's reluctant acceptance of Christianity would provide Hakuchō with a model to emulate in his own behavior. Hakuchō states explicitly that he feels he understands Atsuo better than any other living person.

Hakuchō finally says farewell to Atsuo and returns to Tokyo. There he hears of his death and that A even composed a deathbed poem celebrating his baptism. Hakuchō ends "Autumn" by quoting the poem and reconsidering his assessment of the relative significance of A's baptism for himself and for Hakuchō.

The baptismal water falls gently upon my face;
Sacred water poured on to my head.

It is obvious that even if the baptism were forced upon him, he was somehow or other grateful for it. In that case perhaps A is a more fortunate man than I. (*MHZ*, IV, 592)

Hakuchō is still, as always, hesitant to embrace the Christian religiosity of his brother's death, and this is what pains him, what makes Atsuo more fortunate than he. Still, an important attitude is revealed in the ending of "Autumn." The poetic beauty of not only the baptism but of the entire episode of his brother's death creates an aesthetics of death.

If death becomes a moment of poetry or religious ecstasy, the dying are shielded from the horror of the "ultimate reality." One can get no closer to reality than to view the face of death, unless it is to wear the face of death. For the wizened "realist" Hakuchō, the moment was approaching when the world would know what face he himself would wear.

What does a person feel at the moment of death? I don't know since I've yet to experience it. From of old saints, sages, fools, and idiots have spoken as if they know merely from observation, but they have not understood this "ultimate reality" [*kyūkyoku no shinsō,* literally "true face of finality"]. I wonder whether at the hour of my death I'll follow tradition and custom and intone the *nembutsu* or seek salvation in Christ. (*MHZ,* IV, 590)

IV   *"Elder Brother Rii' (1961)*

Hakuchō's third brother Ritsushi died in October, 1961. "Elder Brother Rii" appeared in *Gunzō* in October, 1961. The events of the story are factual, but the approach is fictional. This is evident from the opening lines.

"Elder Brother Rii dead." When he received the telegram Tetsuzō, the eldest son and heir of the Makimura family, felt not only the conventional sadness but a twinge of relief. Although he was called "Elder Brother Rii," he was the fourth son among the ten Makimura progeny. Because he lived a life of solitude and extreme poverty with no wife, no children, and no regular occupation, after Tokyo became prey to the ravages of war, he returned to the family house in his old home town on the Inland Sea and was living there somehow or other. (*MHZ,* IV, 593)

The "old home town" is Honami, the Makimura family the Masamune family, Tetsuzō Hakuchō, and Elder Brother Rii (a nickname of his own choosing, for Rinzō) Ritsushi. As he had before in such works as "By the Inlet," in the straightforward "Autumn of This Year" Hakuchō mentions that their father had felt he and Ritsushi greatly resembled one another in their basic personalities, and he reiterates this in "Elder Brother Rii."

In the very "fictional" "Rii" Hakuchō even includes a long first-person interior monologue by Rii. In it he describes his unusual physical darkness, a symbol of his eccentricity, his impotence which soon ended his only marriage, and his subsequent hatred of women. The soliloquy is introduced as Tetsuzō wonders whether Rii's spirit is going through the same activities in death as when Rii was alive.

The abject character of Ritsushi offered Hakuchō an especially appropriate topic, in view of Hakuchō's postwar disillusionment with literature. Rii is an artist, a painter. However, he lives in degradation, going some ten years without bathing or cleaning his living area, even tolerating lice, and isolating himself on the second story of the family house he shares in an uneasy arrangement with the old caretaker couple who live downstairs.

His personal filth and uncommunicative eccentricity is imparted to his paintings. Surveying the paintings Rii has left behind, Tetsuzō (Hakuchō) is struck by how incomprehensible and even soiled they are. Tetsuzō wonders, for a moment, if perhaps he simply lacks the ability to appreciate their artistic merit.

Hakuchō ends "Rii" with sentiments that are perhaps directed as much at his own literary career as at the artistic "career" of his reclusive brother. Uemura Tamaki reminded Hakuchō during the prayer meeting at his house the following year, that of his death, that even the greatest writer must humble himself before God. The example of the life and death of his brother "Rii" leaves Hakuchō with the feeling that the greatest writers and artists are also humble before death, that for him as he approaches his own death it is especially absurd to continue thinking of his artistic ambitions.

After joining in passing judgment on Rii's paintings, Tetsuzō, tired from his journey, went to bed early. Suddenly he recalled what his father had said to him long ago, "You are like Rinzō." Then he thought that if he himself had become a painter, perhaps he would have painted paintings like those of Rinzō. If some brilliant judge or critic or foolish judge or critic should appear and heap praise upon their unique charm, perhaps even Rii's paintings would be lauded as those of a Gauguin, van Gogh, or Tessai.

"Don't talk like a fool!" Tetsuzō heard Elder Brother Rii say in his dreams that night. (*MHZ*, IV, 599)

V *In Summary*

Hakuchō's "fear of death" (or, we might say, his "anxiety over the nature of the human condition") dominates the entire sixty years of his thought. Hakuchō's Christianity provided the context, a philosophical framework, in which he discussed his existential concern. Literature was for most of his life the vehicle he found most suitable for commenting upon the nature of human reality; Naturalism was the literary philosophy which freed him from facile assumptions and gave him strength to doubt.

Although the drama of his deathbed conversion is compelling, it came almost as an anticlimax to a long and single-minded literary career that is unique in the history of twentieth-century Japanese literature. Although Hakuchō was never a poor man under severe financial pressure to write, he was never a dilettante, either. He knew that he would never be a Tolstoy or a Dostoyevsky, a Sōseki or an Ōgai, or even a Tōson or a Shūsei, but that was never his purpose. In his writings he sought only to illuminate a corner of reality and to raise the question he almost despaired of ever answering — why?

Titles of Hakuchō's Works Cited

For the reader's convenience, English translations of the titles of Hakuchō's works will be used. The following is an alphabetical list of the Japanese titles and their English equivalents. Also note that the Japanese word order, family name first, is employed throughout this study for Japanese personal names.

"Akumu"	Nightmare
"Anshin"	Peace of Mind
Azuchi no haru	Spring at Azuchi
"Bikō"	Faint Light
"Bungaku seikatsu no rokujūnen"	Sixty Years of Literary Life
"Bungei jihyō"	A Timely Critique of Literature
"Chissoku"	Suffocation
"Dante ni tsuite"	On Dante
"Doko-e"	Whither?
"Doro ningyō"	Clay Doll
Ejima Ikushima	Ejima Ikushima (personal names)
"Hachō heichō"	Discord and Harmony
Himitsu	The Secret
"Hito o koroshita ga"	I Killed a Man, And Yet
"Hito samazama"	Various People
Hitotsu no himitsu	One Secret
"Irie no hotori"	By the Inlet
Iwami Jūtarō	Iwami Jūtarō (personal name)
"Jigoku"	Hell
"Jin'ai"	Dust
Jinsei no kōfuku	The Joys of Life
Kage bōshi	Shadows
Kaigi to shinkō	Doubt and Belief
Kangei sarenu otoko	The Man Who Isn't Welcome
Katsuyori no saigo	The End of Katsuyori
"Kotoshi no aki"	Autumn of This Year
"Kotoshi no haru"	Spring This Year
"Kotoshi no shoka"	Early Summer This Year
Kumo no kanata e	Beyond the Clouds

156

"Kyūyū"   Old Friend
"Machibito kitarazu"   The Caller Didn't Come
"Meimō"   Illusion
Mitsuhide to Jōha   Mitsuhide and Jōha
"Natsume Sōseki-ron"   A Study of Natsume Sōseki
"Nenashigusa"   Duckweed
"Nihon dasshutsu"   Escape from Japan
"Nikai no mado"   The Second-story Window
"Ningengirai"   The Misanthrope
"Rii anisan" (also "Rii aasan")   Elder Brother Rii
"Sekibaku"   Solitude
Shinda yō na heiwa   A Death-like Peace
"Shinjū misui"   Attempted Double Suicide
Shirakabe   White Wall
"Shisha seija"   The Dead and the Living
"Shizenshugi bungaku seisuishi"   A History of the Rise and Fall of
                                            Naturalist Literature
"Suimin'yaku o nomu made"   Until He Takes the Sleeping
                                            Medicine
Tenshi hokaku   Capture the Angel
"Torō"   Wasted Effort
"Torusutoi ni tsuite"   On Tolstoy
"Uchimura Kanzō"   Uchimura Kanzō (personal name)
"Ushibeya no nioi"   The Smell of the Cowshed
"Yōkaiga"   Ghost Picture

Notes and References

Abbreviations:
MHZ *Masamune Hakuchō zenshū* (The Complete Works of Masamune Hakuchō), 13 volumes (Tokyo: Shinchōsha, 1965–1966).
MN *Monumenta Nipponica*
WB *Waseda Bungaku*
SS *Shinshōsetsu*

Chapter One

1. Ōiwa Kō, *Masamune Hakuchō-ron* (Tokyo: Satsuki Shobō, 1966), p. 31.
2. Yamamoto Kenkichi, *Masamune Hakuchō: sono soko ni aru mono* (Tokyo: Bungei Shunjū, 1975), p. 29.
3. Gotō Ryō, *Masamune Hakuchō; bungaku to shōgai* (Tokyo: Shichōsha, 1966), p. 26.
4. Ibid., p. 32.
5. Ibid., p. 32.
6. Ōiwa, p. 193.
7. Ibid., pp. 193–194.
8. Gotō, p. 45.
9. Ibid., p. 46.
10. Ibid., p. 48.
11. Ibid., p. 50.
12. Ōiwa, pp. 106–107.
13. Gotō, p. 58.
14. See Ōiwa, pp. 57–59, Gotō, pp. 59–60.
15. Harry Levin, *The Gates of Horn: A Study of Five French Realists* (New York: Oxford, 1966), p. 72.
16. Gotō, p. 91.
17. See, for example, Gotō, 71.
18. Gotō, p. 100.
19. Ibid., p. 110.
20. Ibid., p. 118.
21. Introducing novels through newspaper and magazine serialization is still common in Japan. Despite Hakuchō's misgivings in 1908, in later years Natsume Sōseki and Tanizaki Jun'ichirō, among others, first published major novels in this way.

22. Gotō, pp. 145–146. Gotō quotes from Hakuchō's "Shimbun to bungaku" (Newspapers and literature), *Bunshō Sekai,* August, 1908.
23. Ibid., p. 206.
24. Ibid., pp. 204–205.
25. George Oakley Totten III, *The Social Democratic Movement in Prewar Japan* (New Haven: Yale Univ. Press, 1966), pp. 65–66.
26. Ibid., pp. 414, 416.
27. Gotō, pp. 264–267.
28. Ibid., pp. 280–281.
29. Ibid., pp. 348–350.
30. Ibid., pp. 292–293.
31. Ōiwa, p. 71.
32. Hyōdō Masanosuke, *Masamune Hakuchō-ron* (Tokyo: Keisō Shobō, 1968), pp. 195–200.
33. Ibid., pp. 229, 233–234.
34. Ōiwa, p. 230.
35. Gotō, pp. 319–320.
36. Ōiwa, pp. 228–229.
37. Gotō, pp. 321–322.
38. Ibid., pp. 324–325.
39. Ōiwa, p. 225.
40. Uemura Tamaki, "Masamune Hakuchō sensei o omou," *Fujin no Tomo,* December, 1962, p. 183.
41. Ibid., p. 183.

Chapter Two

1. Ōiwa, p. 87.
2. Gotō, pp. 66–67.
3. *MHZ,* I, 28.
4. "Hachō Heichō," *SS,* February, 1906, p. 147.
5. Ōiwa, p. 120.
6. Ibid., pp. 121–122.
7. Ibid., p. 123.
8. "Nikai no mado," *WB,* August, 1906, p. 126.
9. "Kyūyū," *SS,* September, 1906, p. 52.
10. Ōiwa, p. 126.
11. "Kyūyū," p. 15.
12. Ibid., p. 18.
13. Marcus Dods, *The Book of Genesis* (New York, 1901). On page 6 of "Kyūyū" Hakuchō has referred specifically to "Dods' commentary on Genesis."
14. "Kyūyū," p. 7.
15. *Meiji shisōka no shūkyō-kan,* ed. Hikakushisōshi Kenkyūkai (Tokyo: Daizō, 1975), p. 203.

16. Ogasawara Masatoshi, "Uchimura no mukyōkaishugi to Pyūritani-zumu," *Gendai ni ikiru Uchimura Kanzō,* ed. by Kyōbunkan (Tokyo: Kyōbunkan, 1976), p. 212.

17. Ibid., p. 214.

18. "Kyūyū," p. 21.

19. *Shizenshugi bungaku seisuishi, MHZ,* XII, 315-316. Hakuchō cites Hōgetsu's essay "Kaigi to kokuhaku" (Doubt and Confession).

20. "Kyūyū," pp. 29-30.

21. "Dust," trans. Robert Rolf, *MN,* XXV (1970), p. 407.

22. Ōiwa feels Hakuchō changed from a "Realistic" to an "Existential" writer when he moved to Ōiso in 1921 (p. 141).

23. "Dust," p. 414.

24. Ibid., p. 414.

25. See *MHZ,* I, 37.

26. "Anshin," *Shumi,* June, 1907, p. 134.

27. Ibid., pp. 137-138.

Chapter Three

1. Francis Mathy, *Shiga Naoya* (New York: Twayne, 1974), p. 74.

2. William F. Sibley, "Naturalism in Japanese Literature," *Harvard Journal of Asiatic Studies,* 28 (1968), 169.

3. Beongcheon Yu, *Natsume Sōseki* (New York: Twayne, 1969), p. 21.

4. Arnold Hauser, trans. Stanley Godman, *The Social History of Art,* IV (New York: Vintage Books, 1958), p. 65.

5. "Idea fiction" (also known as *"shisō shōsetsu"* — literally "thought fiction" — and *"tēma shōsetsu,"* "theme fiction") attempted to uplift by fictionalization of an idea or moral; flourished a few years after 1895; its major exponents were Kawakami Bizan (1869–1908) and Izumi Kyōka (1873–1939).

6. Nakamura Mitsuo, *Fūzoku shōsetsuron* (Tokyo: Shinchōsha, 1958), p. 31.

7. At the same time, however, it has also been viewed as "the first step in the direction of the autobiographical novel." See Mathy, op. cit., p. 35.

8. Nakamura, p. 46.

9. See Yoshida Seiichi & Wada Kingo, eds. *Kindai bungaku hyōron taikei,* Vol. 3 (Tokyo: Kadokawa Shoten, 1972), pp. 417-431. The nine *"Futon gappyō"* contributors were: Oguri Fūyō, Matsuhara Shibun, Katakami Noburu, Mizuno Yōshū, Tokuda Shūkō, Nakamura Seiko, Sōma Gyofū, Shimamura Hōgetsu, and Hakuchō.

10. Yoshida Seiichi, *Shizenshugi no kenkyū,* II (Tokyo: Tokyo-dō, 1958), pp. 160-161.

11. Hirano Ken, *Sakkaron-shū* (Tokyo: Shinchōsha, 1971), p. 58. From his "Tokuda Shūsei" (October, 1969).

12. In 1906 Katai said he was no longer going to write Romantic stories

and that he was going to begin depicting reality as it was. In September, 1907, he stated that in order to "touch" reality the writer must objectively portray reality as it is, but that he will fail if he is too distant from the reality he is portraying. See *Shizenshugi no kenkyū,* II, 152–155.

13. *"Futon* gappyō," *WB,* October, 1907, p. 41.
14. Gotō, p. 81.
15. Ibid., p. 83.
16. Ibid., p. 81.
17. Ōiwa, p. 172.
18. Ibid., p. 172.
19. Ibid., p. 140.
20. Even the conservative Mori Ōgai was forced into action by the extremes of the Meiji government's restrictions on free speech. See "Mori Ōgai's Response to Suppression of Intellectual Freedom, 1909–1912," *MN,* XXIX (1974), 381–413, by Helen M. Hopper. Apparently the exact criteria of the Press Laws "used to decide whether or not publications" were "corruptive of public morals" were vague (p. 394). No explicit references to human sexual relations were tolerated, which certainly restricted the Naturalist writer in his attempt to re-create reality. That the Naturalists were considered the chief literary corrupters of public morals goes without saying, which led to the ironic turn of events whereby Ōgai's novel *Vita Sexualis,* parodying those of the Naturalists, was suppressed by the government because of its Naturalism. Hopper notes, "Ōgai's novella was branded 'naturalistic' and therefore 'subversive' and potentially 'corruptive' to the 'common people' and subject to be 'killed.' " Ōgai was thus "condemned as a purveyor of 'dangerous thoughts' " (p. 387). In this context see Hopper, pp. 381, 386–387, 394, 397–398.
21. Curiously, Hakuchō's reputation as a nihilist somehow made him suspect as an anarchist in the minds of authorities perhaps a bit unsure of their "isms." Hakuchō was put under surveillance by the Tokyo Metropolitan Police and followed during the period of the Kōtoku Shūsui Incident from the fall of 1910 until January, 1911. On the day of Shūsui's execution Hakuchō was confined to his home by the police. His reputation as a nihilist made him suspect as an anarchist although he had no connection with Shūsui and had given no indication that he was one of his followers in any way. See Gotō, p. 89.
22. Gotō, p. 92.
23. Ibid., p. 90.
24. *Shizenshugi bungaku seisuishi, MHZ,* XII, 376.
25. Gotō, p. 93.
26. Egawa uses the English "hospitable": "hosupitaburu."

Chapter Four

1. *Chūō Kōron,* a prestigious monthly devoted to social and political

commentary and the arts; Hakuchō was a frequent contributor all his life from 1904.

2. Ōiwa, pp. 137–138.

3. Kumbhira: associated especially with Kagawa Prefecture on Shikoku; revered by seafarers as a patron deity of safe passage.

4. Gotō, p. 129.

5. Ibid., p. 138.

6. Ibid., p. 139.

7. I Corinthians 13:1 (King James Version).

8. Genesis 1:22 (King James Version).

9. Burton Watson, *Cold Mountain* (New York: Columbia Univ. Press), p. 68.

10. Philipp Mainlaender (pseudonym for Philipp Batz), 1841–1876.

11. See Gotō, p. 172, and Ōiwa, pp. 146, 150.

12. Ōiwa, p. 187.

13. Mori Ōgai, "Mōsō," (Delusion), trans. John W. Dower, *MN,* XXV (1970), 430.

14. Ibid., p. 429.

15. Yamamoto Kenkichi notes (p. 34) that after leaving Christianity Hakuchō used logic to ridicule the Bible so vehemently that Uchimura referred to Hakuchō as a "devil" (*akuma*).

16. See "Waga ichinichi no kōdō," *MHZ,* XI, 338.

17. His mother could be viewed in a Freudian sense as the first cause of his impotence. She is possessive, pampering, and over-protective. It is she who gained the most satisfaction from the departure of Tamotsu's wife, and she who most opposes his desires to be reunited with his former wife.

Chapter Five

1. Henry Francis Cary, *The Vision of Dante Alighieri: or Hell Purgatory and Paradise* (London, 1923), p. 22.

2. Ibid., p. 201.

3. Ibid., p. 370.

4. Ibid., p. 389. I omit Hakuchō's quote of Paradise, XXI, 106–113.

5. Ōiwa, pp. 67, 71.

6. Gotō, p. 294.

7. Ōiwa, pp. 76–77.

8. Ibid., p. 72.

9. Ibid., p. 76.

10. Ibid., p. 21.

11. Uchimura's feelings of persecution arose from the "Disrespect Incident." On January 19, 1891, before an assembly of a thousand middle school students and sixty fellow faculty members, Uchimura, the only Christian faculty member present, for reasons of both Christian conscience and simple unfamiliarity with the ceremony, failed to bow before

the Emperor's signature on an imperial rescript. For this he was rebuked as a traitor and lost his teaching position. A brief but informative account of this incident is in *Bundan shiji-ten,* Hasegawa Izumi (Tokyo: Shibundō, 1972), pp. 19–20.

12. Gotō, p. 220.
13. Ibid., p. 221.
14. Ibid., p. 220.
15. Ibid., p. 215.
16. William Flint Thrall & Addison Hibbard, *A Handbook to Literature* (New York: Odyssey, 1960), p. 310.
17. Ōiwa, pp. 167–168.
18. Gotō, p. 211.

Chapter Six

1. Gotō, pp. 177–178.
2. Ibid., pp. 178–179.
3. The six original members of *Kaze* were: Hamada Sumiko, Hanagata Keiko, Ishibashi Kenji, Matsumura Hikojirō, Noda Yūji, and Shinohara Daisaku. The first director and an important force in *Kaze's* creation as a vehicle for Hakuchō's plays was Yamada Hajime. Hamada, Ishibashi, Matsumura, and Noda are still with *Kaze.*
4. Gotō, pp. 177, 179.
5. "Kumo no kanata e," *Kaizō,* August, 1925, p. 14.
6. Ibid., p. 19.
7. Ibid., p. 26.
8. Gotō, p. 187.
9. Ibid., pp. 313–315.
10. The healing Bodhisattva.
11. A shrewd politician, he later secured the patronage of Hideyoshi.
12. The Taikō is Hideyoshi. For "Ehon Taikō-ki" see *The Kabuki Handbook,* A.S. & G.M. Halford (Tokyo: Tuttle, 1956), pp. 22–25, 467–468.
13. "Iwami Jūtarō," *Bungei Shunjū,* March, 1935, p. 362.
14. See *Buke Hennen Jiten,* ed. Inagaki Shisei (Tokyo: Seiabō, 1968), pp. 357–359.

Chapter Seven

1. Kitamori Kazō, *Nihon no kokoro to Kirisuto-kyō* (Tokyo: Yomiuri Shimbun-sha, 1973), pp. 174–180.

Selected Bibliography

PRIMARY SOURCES

1. Hakuchō's works cited:

"Anshin." *Shumi,* June, 1907, pp. 132–138.
"*Futon* gappyō." *Waseda Bungaku,* October, 1907, p. 41.
"Hachō heichō." *Shinshōsetsu,* February, 1906, pp. 107–148.
"Iwami Jūtarō." *Bungei Shunjū,* March, 1935, pp. 352–365.
"Kumo no kanata e." *Kaizō,* August, 1925, pp. 1–34.
"Kyūyū." *Shinshōsetsu,* September, 1906, pp. 1–52.
Masamune Hakuchō zenshū. 13 vols. Tokyo: Shinchōsha, 1965–66.
"Nikai no mado." *Waseda Bungaku,* August, 1906, pp. 125–137.

2. Hakuchō's Works in English:

"Doro ningyō." "The Mud Doll." Tr. by Gregg M. Sinclair and Kazo Suita. *Tokyo People: Three Stories from the Japanese.* Tokyo: Keibunkan, 1925, pp. 119–233.
"Jin'ai." "Dust." Tr. by Robert Rolf. *Monumenta Nipponica,* XXV, 1970, pp. 407–414.
"New Light on Lafcadio Hearn." *Contemporary Japan,* September, 1933, pp. 270–280.

SECONDARY SOURCES

1. In Japanese:

FUKUDA, KIYOTO AND SASAKI, TŌRU. *Masamune Hakuchō: hito to sakuhin,* Century Books no. 24. Tokyo: Shimizu Shoin, 1967. A little book, but of use as a brief introduction to Hakuchō.
GOTŌ, RYŌ. *Masamune Hakuchō: bungaku to shōgai.* Tokyo: Shichōsha, 1966. Complete, readable biography; an essential work on Hakuchō. Contains entertaining account of Hakuchō's first trip to the West.
HYŌDŌ, MASANOSUKE. *Masamune Hakuchō-ron.* Tokyo: Keisō Shobō, 1968. Intelligent discussion of such areas as Hakuchō's nihilism; has important reference bibliography of works on Hakuchō from 1908 to 1968.
Kaze: Pneuma. Tiny magazine-program published by *Kaze.* Sixteen issues from October, 1963, to October, 1974. See early issues for reflections

on Hakuchō of Masamune Tsune, Nakamura Mitsuo, Yamamoto Kenkichi, and Yoshida Seiichi.

KITAMORI, KAZŌ. *Nihon no kokoro to Kirisuto-kyō.* Tokyo: Yomiuri Shimbun-sha, 1973, pp. 174–180. A theologian discusses Hakuchō's Christianity.

NODA, YŪJI. "Ganshū no engekijin." *Higeki Kigeki,* Special Issue on Taishō Drama, no. 2. December, 1976, pp. 19–27. Discussion of Hakuchō's plays by one who actually directs them.

ŌIWA, KŌ. *Masamune Hakuchō-ron.* Tokyo: Satsuki Shobō, 1966. Valuable insider's view of Hakuchō by a postwar acquaintance. Brief and extremely sympathetic, but displays understanding of Hakuchō's Christianity. A necessary companion to the Gotō volume.

TANABE, AKIO. *Hyōden: Masamune Hakuchō.* Tokyo: Gakugei Shorin, 1977. Latest study of Hakuchō; some new thoughts and new directions but slightly uncritical; useful as an introduction.

UEMURA, TAMAKI. "Masamune Hakuchō sensi o omou." *Fujin no Tomo,* December, 1962, pp. 182–183. Uemura's testimony that Hakuchō died a Christian.

YAMAMOTO, KENKICHI. *Masamune Hakuchō: sono soko ni aru mono.* Tokyo: Bungei Shunjū, 1975. Twenty-two essays that appeared monthly in *Bungakkai* from September, 1969, to February, 1970, and frequently from January, 1971, to November, 1973. Intelligent commentary by a noted critic. Imaginative, fruitful discussions, such as comparisons of Hakuchō and Evelyn Waugh. Marred only by lengthy accounts of internecine squabbles between Yamamoto and Gotō Ryō.

YOSHIDA, SEIICHI. *Shizenshugi no kenkyū.* 2 vols. Tokyo: Tokyo-dō, 1955, 1958. Huge study of Naturalism with several chapters devoted to Hakuchō.

2. Studies of Hakuchō in English:

ROLF, ROBERT. "Shūsei, Hakuchō, and the Age of Literary Naturalism, 1907–1911." Diss. University of Hawaii, 1975. Pages 91–317 contain a complete biography of Hakuchō and a study of his Naturalistic stories of the years 1907–1911.

SIBLEY, WILLIAM F. "Naturalism in Japanese Literature." *Harvard Journal of Asiatic Studies,* 28, 1968, pp. 157–169. Concise, comprehensive essay on Naturalism with frequent reference to Hakuchō.

Index

Akechi Mitsuhide, 133, 135-37
Akutagawa Ryūnosuke, 52
Analects, The (Confucius), 131
Arajotai (Shūsei), 63, 86-88
autobiographical fiction, 23, 24-25, 26-27, 28, 60-62, 76-78

Balzac, Honore de, 21, 121
Bible, 16, 17, 18, 19, 20, 27, 33, 45, 48, 66, 68, 71, 91, 92-93, 95, 102, 131
Boccaccio, 33, 114
Botan dōrō, 82, 93, 145
Buddhism, 15-16, 25, 45-50, 71, 77, 87, 89, 96, 101, 102, 103, 106, 107, 117, 130, 133, 145, 146-47, 148-50
Bungakkai, 17
Bungei-za, 125
"Byōshō nisshi" (Masamune Tsune), 37-38
Byron, George Gordon, 92

Calvinism, 48, 56
Carlyle, Thomas, 18, 19, 111-12, 120
Cary, Henry Francis, 111, 120
Cervantes, 19
Chekhov, Anton, 126
Chikamatsu Monzaemon, 20
Chikamatsu Shūkō, 26, 32, 72, 73
China, 30-31
Chūō Kōron, 28, 35, 86, 122, 126, 148, 150, 162-63n1
Christianity, 16, 17, 18, 19-20, 33, 35, 36-38, 39, 40, 45-50, 56-58, 65, 67, 68, 70-72, 91, 96, 97-98, 101-103, 106, 107, 111-20, 121, 125, 128, 130-32, 133, 146-48, 150-53, 155, 163n15, 163-64 n11
Coleridge, Samuel Taylor, 92
Confucianism, 100, 131
Crane, Stephen, 73

Dainiji Geijutsu-za, 125

Dante, 16, 18, 19, 27, 28, 30, 33, 66, 97, 98, 99, 102, 111-24, 128
Decameron, The (Boccaccio), 33
Divine Comedy, The (Dante), 16, 28, 33, 100, 102, 111-24
Doppo: See Kunikida Doppo
Doppo-shū (Doppo), 22
Dostoyevsky, 35, 121, 155
Dreiser, Theodore, 69

Ehon Taikō-ki, 137
Existentialism, 51-52, 55, 60, 107

Flaubert, Gustave, 59, 63
folklore, 144
Forty-seven Rōnin, The, 142
Futabatei Shimei, 61, 66
Futon (Katai), 23, 61-63
"*Futon* gappyō", 62, 161n9

Genji Monogatari, 121
"Getsuyō bungaku," 21
Gibbon, Edward, 37
Goethe, Johann, 18, 19, 112, 120, 122
Goncourt Brothers, Edmond and Jules, 73
Grandgent, C.H., 112
Greek mythology, 97, 100
Gunzō, 141, 153

Haiyūza, 143
Hakai (Tōson), 22, 61, 161n7
Hakkenden (Bakin), 33, 120
Han Shan, 97, 100
Haru (Tōson), 63
Hatsu sugata (Kosugi Tengai), 62-63
Hawthorne, Nathaniel, 127
Heike Monogatari, 120, 134
Hero of Our Time, A (Lermontov), 63-64
Hideyoshi: See Tokutomi Hideyoshi
Homer, 18, 27

167